Henry VIII

The story of the ruthless Tudor king

Henry VIII

The story of the ruthless Tudor king

HARRIET CASTOR

A & C Black • London

First published 2010 by
A & C Black Publishers Ltd
36 Soho Square, London, W1D 3QY

www.acblack.com

Text copyright © 2010 Harriet Castor

The right of Harriet Castor to be identified as the author
of this work has been asserted by her in accordance with
the Copyrights, Designs and Patents Act 1988.

ISBN 978-1-4081-1323-3

A CIP catalogue for this book is available from the British Library.

This book is produced using paper that is made from wood grown in
managed, sustainable forests. It is natural, renewable and recyclable.
The logging and manufacturing processes conform to the
environmental regulations of the country of origin.

Printed and bound in Great Britain
by CPI Cox & Wyman, Reading RG1 8EX.

1

It was bitterly, bone-achingly cold. But still the people had turned out – had been waiting for hours, stamping their feet, jostling, arguing and joking. Inside St Paul's, the old cathedral was more packed than Smithfield on market day. Outside, crowds thronged the churchyard and the streets beyond, hanging from windows and teetering on rooftops – risking their necks for a sight of royalty. It was the day of a royal wedding.

'Hey, look! They're coming outside!'

At the far side of the cathedral yard, the doors of the Bishop's Palace were opening. A procession was forming, at its centre, a young couple. The sight of them drew gasps. No English brides wore veils covering their faces. But this bride was a Spanish princess, dressed in shimmering white, her face concealed by a jewelled veil that reached to her waist.

The boy was equally stunning. Tall for his age, already built like an athlete, and wearing fantastically expensive clothes and jewels, he looked magnificent, and he knew it. It was a shame he wasn't the groom, perhaps. It was a shame *his* job was just to escort the bride to his older brother.

Ten-year-old Henry, Duke of York, second son of the king and queen, was concentrating too hard to think of such things. He knew all eyes were on him, and he loved the attention, but he also knew he could not put a foot wrong. At a stately, dignified pace, he led the Spanish princess, Catherine of Aragon, across the yard to the cathedral's mighty west doors.

Inside, as a trumpet fanfare echoed up to the stone-vaulted roof, they mounted a flight of steps. It was like climbing onto a theatre stage – a walkway had been built at head-height, which ran the entire length of the nave. At its mid-point was a platform, where Henry's older brother was waiting for his bride.

Prince Arthur was fifteen – pale and slight where Henry was sturdy, serious where Henry was all golden smiles. But what he lacked in charisma, he made up for in importance. Arthur was the future King of England.

Henry stepped back as the ceremony began, and glanced upwards. Faces looked down on him from every possible vantage point. But the two faces he cared about most – his parents' – he could not see. They were hidden behind the glazed windows of the specially built royal box.

His mother would be watching him, he knew, with her usual warm, indulgent smile. But his father… Henry thought of that severe, gaunt face and shivered. His father would reserve his smiles for Arthur.

He was right. In the royal box, King Henry VII was watching his eldest son. Young Henry and his sisters, Margaret and Mary, hardly registered for him today. This was a moment of triumph for the king. His family, the Tudors, was being joined in marriage to one of the oldest and most powerful royal dynasties of Europe, the kings and queens of Spain. This would give them powerful allies – and it would help secure Arthur's position as heir to the throne.

LIVESinACTION

Arthur was the boy the king's dreams rested on. After his own death, a new age would dawn. The golden age of Arthur, the second great Tudor king.

2

The horse's hooves struck sparks from the stones of the outer courtyard at Greenwich Palace as the messenger raced in. The man pulled up the reins savagely.

'Where is His Grace, the king?' he asked, jumping down from the saddle and flinging the reins to a groom. 'My message is urgent!'

Escorted – almost running – to the palace's inner courtyard, the messenger plunged through a doorway and up the stairs to the Watching Chamber, where the royal guards stood on duty.

There were quick discussions. Then the messenger was shown through into the Presence

Chamber. He bowed to the canopied throne, even though it stood empty, and spoke in low tones to one of the councillors waiting beside it.

The councillor looked stricken. He dismissed the messenger and said to his colleagues, 'The king must be told immediately. But who will do it?'

'I will,' said a man, stepping forward. It was the king's confessor, a brown-robed friar.

A moment later, the friar knelt before the king.

'Your Grace, forgive my intrusion,' he said. 'Those whom God blesses, God also asks to bear a heavy burden.'

The king, who was in the middle of supper, froze. His eyes were cold and fearful. 'What do you mean, "heavy burden"? What has happened? Tell me!'

'A messenger has arrived from Ludlow,' said the friar gently. 'Your son Prince Arthur has succumbed to his fever. He is dead.'

The great howl of grief that followed echoed through the palace. Then came the sound of running feet. A servant raced to the queen's apartment.

'Fetch the queen! Quickly! His Grace has collapsed! He needs her –'

A few moments later, Queen Elizabeth reached her husband's room. She dismissed everyone else and took him in her arms like a child.

Between wracking sobs, the king spoke brokenly of his heir ... of the crown ... of all his hopes, lost.

At last, Elizabeth said, 'Do not despair, my dearest lord. Remember, we have another son – we have Henry.'

Henry! The king knew his wife had always favoured the boy, but he was no match for Arthur. Besides, he might die, too.

'One life is fragile!' he said. 'One son is not enough!'

'But you were your mother's only son,' Elizabeth reminded him. '*You* survived. And we are both young. We can have more children.'

Later, when the king was quiet and she had given him over to the care of his servants, Elizabeth walked grimly back to her own rooms. It was only when she was in the privacy of her bedchamber, with the door closed, that she broke down.

Her younger son's rooms were in the same wing of the palace. Little Henry had heard the commotion, the hurrying feet; he had looked through his windows into the courtyard, hoping for an explanation, but had seen nothing. Now, faintly but distinctly, he could hear his mother crying. It was more than he could bear.

'Let me go to her!' he cried, twisting his arm out of his nurse's grip. 'I command it, or it shall be the worse for you!'

Although he was only ten, that was a threat of some force. The nurse gave way. The ladies guarding the door of Elizabeth's chamber did the same.

'Mama,' said Henry, entering the room quietly. 'What is wrong?'

Elizabeth looked up, her face swollen with crying. 'My boy… My darling… Poor Arthur has died. You, my sweetheart – you are heir to the throne now.' She gathered Henry to her and rocked him gently. 'One day you will be King.'

3

The crown of England was a diadem dripping with blood. It was a prize that King Henry VII had seized violently. At the Battle of Bosworth Field in 1485, his soldiers had killed the old king, Richard III. They had grabbed Richard's crown and placed it on Henry's head right there on the battlefield. This was the final act in a terrifying and brutal civil war that had lasted, on and off, for more than thirty years.

The Battle of Bosworth had been sixteen years ago. Now King Henry VII was forty-four years old. Under his magnificent robes he was a thin, wiry man, battle-hardened and determined. The royal family before him – the Plantagenets – had reigned for more than three hundred years. Many people said that Henry and his family – the Tudors – were upstarts, and that they would soon be overthrown. Henry had worked tirelessly to prove them wrong.

His claim to the throne, which came through his mother's family, was shaky. There were nobles at Court who had more royal blood running in their veins than he did. They were a danger to him – so he had many of them executed. When there were uprisings and rebellions, Henry rode into battle again, and crushed them.

After all that bloodshed, he would not let the Tudor dynasty die for lack of an heir. One son was not enough. It would only take a fever, a fall from a horse – or even a crossbow bolt from an assassin's weapon – and his dream of a long line of Tudor kings would be finished. So Queen Elizabeth had to have another child.

And soon she became pregnant. The king was overjoyed, hoping it would be a boy. But tragedy was about to strike again.

4

The White Tower is the most ancient part of the Tower of London. It is not a single tower, but a huge, thick-walled fortress with turrets on its roof and dungeons in its bowels. Inside its upper storey there is a chapel, ancient and beautiful, carved out of the cold stone like a tomb.

On a bitter February day in 1503, the young Henry knelt in that chapel, his hands pressed together in prayer. The great stained-glass windows were covered with black cloth, but the chapel was a blaze of golden flickering light. A thousand fine wax candles were burning. And in their midst, awful to look upon, lay a coffin.

Elizabeth's baby had been born – not the son the king wanted, but a little girl, Katherine. However, the baby had not lived long. And Elizabeth herself had become feverish, as was always the danger after childbirth. A few days later, on her thirty-seventh birthday, she had died.

To her eleven-year-old son, the days since her death had been a living nightmare. Henry had grown up in his mother's care – she had been the centre of his life; a life of laughter, warmth and love. Now that love was gone, and there was nothing to replace it.

Henry had not wept for Arthur, ten months before. He had hardly known his brother. But he was weeping now.

5

The rain had been dripping all morning on the palace of Richmond, adding a glistening sheen to its fairy-tale turrets. Henry, heir to the throne of England, fifteen years old now, was striding down the passageway leading to the Privy Chamber. Seeing the prince's expression, the guards who were stationed outside the door uncrossed their halberds hurriedly to let him pass.

'What is this, Father?' said Henry, bursting into the room. 'They tell me I cannot joust in the tournament next week!'

The king glanced up briefly from his accounts ledger, his finger marking his place. 'I am busy.'

Henry was not put off. 'Every minute of every day I face nothing but rules and restrictions,' he said. 'I am a prince, not a tethered animal!'

With a grimace, the king put down his quill. As he looked at the well-muscled, broad-shouldered youth before him, he was aware of the contrast between them. He was greyer and thinner now than he had ever been, and hours spent hunched over the royal accounts had made him stoop. He resented not just his son's health, but his spirit – Henry's quickness to laugh, his popularity.

'I will keep you safe at all costs,' said the king. 'There are plenty who would love to take the crown from us. Do not help them.'

'But, Father – great kings must be great warriors!' said Henry. 'You won the crown on the battlefield. And you have faced armies. You *must* let me joust!'

Jousting was Henry's favourite sport – a war game fought on horseback with lethal spears called lances. It was excellent training for battle, but it was highly dangerous. Men often made their wills before entering a jousting tournament.

'Must?' The king raised his eyebrows. 'The risk is too great. I will not have you dead for a sport!'

Henry walked forward and leant on his father's desk. 'But you *will* let me be humiliated,' he said. 'While all the young men at Court take part, I must sit and watch like a child! You would not have said this to Arthur.'

There was an icy pause. The king's chair scraped against the floor as he stood up.

'*Never* mention his name,' he said. 'And stop this foolish bravado. When you are king, you will understand. You will fear for the succession, too.'

Henry laughed scornfully. 'Look at me! Do you doubt for one moment that I will have strong sons?'

For several moments, the king's gaze was steady, but he did not speak. Then he sat down and dipped his quill in a pot of ink. 'Get out of my sight,' he said crisply. He did not look up.

Henry turned on his heel and strode out.

As the months passed, the king became obsessed with keeping his family's grip on the throne. He was convinced that the powerful nobles at Court would try to prevent his son from succeeding.

Growing suspicious of everyone, he decided to exercise control through money. He charged the nobles huge fines for any behaviour he did not like. Those who stepped out of line were ruined, and their lands seized. The king – counting the confiscated riches as they clinked into his coffers – came to be seen as a money-grabbing miser.

But when at last his health began to fail, he became afraid that God would judge him harshly for his actions – for his greed, and for all those who had been killed on his order.

Terrified of death, the king hid himself away more and more in his private apartments, and the Court became a place of dark shadows and whispers.

Henry knew he would be a different kind of ruler. He only had to wait ... wait until the power was his. Wait until he was King.

6

The guards outside the Presence Chamber jumped as a crack of loud laughter rang out. Beyond the heavy carved doors, the new king was sitting in his richly upholstered, gold-fringed chair, talking with a group of courtiers.

'And what say you, Lord Mountjoy?' asked Henry, turning to one of his favourite advisors.

'Your Grace, this is the dawn of a golden age.' William Blount, Lord Mountjoy, stepped forward and knelt before his young sovereign. 'It is the end of sadness, the beginning of joy. You are a king who does not desire gold or gems or precious metals, but virtue, glory and everlasting fame!'

Henry laughed again and stood up, taking the man by the shoulders and raising him, too. 'William, you flatter us!' he said. 'But you have our aims aright. With God's help, this will be a golden age indeed.'

It was May 1 1509, and the old king had died just one week before. Henry had become King Henry VIII of England. And he was not yet eighteen years old.

'We *do* desire glory,' Henry continued, looking towards the river, where brightly decorated barges were taking part in the May Day celebrations. 'A warrior king's glory. We shall reclaim our birthright, William – we shall conquer France. And we shall have many fine sons to succeed us.' Henry turned from the window, his face as sunny as the scene outside. 'William, I have a vision – the Tudor line will reign for a thousand years!'

Throughout the land, the people were rejoicing. Young Henry was everyone's idea of what a king should be – tall, strong, handsome and clever. Gone were the old king's miserly policies. Gone were his most-hated money-grabbing councillors – they were in prison, awaiting execution.

Henry wanted his new Court to be a glittering centre of learning, chivalry and talent. He wanted to surround himself with brave knights and great scholars, be entertained by the finest musicians and have his palaces decorated by the greatest artists and craftsmen of the age. And he needed a queen at his side, to preside over his Court and to give him many healthy children.

Now the door to the Presence Chamber opened. One of Henry's servants entered and made a low bow. 'Your Grace, the astrologer begs leave to attend you.'

'Show him in,' said Henry, settling back into his great chair.

The astrologer approached Henry's throne and knelt.

'So,' said Henry, 'you have consulted your charts? Tell me the most favourable date for my coronation.'

'By my calculations, Your Grace,' said the astrologer, unrolling a large piece of parchment, 'it is Midsummer's Day – June 24.'

Henry scanned the chart and nodded. 'That pleases me well.' He looked round at his advisors. 'It shall be a joint coronation – with my queen.'

As the astrologer retreated, one of Henry's advisors stepped forward. 'Ah, yes, Your Grace, I have a list here of suitable candidates for marriage.' He held out a paper. 'I beg humbly to suggest …

Your Grace might consider a French princess?'

As Henry knew, a royal marriage was a political matter. It was a way to make an alliance with another country. France was one of the most powerful countries in Europe … and one of England's oldest enemies.

'No, I will have no French woman,' he said, waving away the list. 'I do not want to maintain peace with France, sir. As I told Lord Mountjoy, I want to *invade* it! Besides, I have made my choice.'

'Princess Catherine?' asked the advisor.

The other great power in Europe was Spain. If Henry made friends with the Spanish king, they could attack France together. Marrying a Spanish princess was a good first step. And Princess Catherine, Arthur's widow, still lived in England.

'Of course Princess Catherine!' said Henry impatiently. 'Don't look so worried. Catherine is descended from great kings. She's pretty, too.' He rose and clapped the man on the shoulder. 'She will give me many sons, you'll see.'

'But, Your Grace, she is your brother's widow. Are there not doubts as to whether the Church permits such a marriage?'

Henry VIII

Henry waved a dismissive hand. 'It has all been dealt with. Pope Julius has already given us a dispensation.'

The Pope was head of the Church in Europe, and even kings were supposed to obey him. Because Catherine had been married to Henry's brother, Henry needed special permission – a dispensation – from the Pope to marry her. Fortunately, one of these had been issued after Arthur's death.

So Henry and Catherine became husband and wife. And on Midsummer's Day 1509, they were crowned in Westminster Abbey in London. Henry commanded that the celebrations should be the finest England had ever seen. He loved having fun. And now he was King, the fun and celebration could last as long as he wished.

7

In a day's hunting, Henry could exhaust eight or ten horses. He was a great shot with a bow, an agile and strong wrestler, a fine tennis player, and he had first ridden a full-sized warhorse – alone in the saddle – in a procession through London at the age of three.

Henry was six foot two, with red-gold hair and blue eyes, a skilled musician and composer, a graceful and energetic dancer, and a keen gambler at dice and cards. Best of all, he liked the combat sports his father had forbidden. However, even now he was king, Henry hesitated to take part without an heir to replace him. It was frustrating to sit and watch others joust, but Henry believed that soon Catherine would give him a son.

Catherine's first pregnancy ended in miscarriage, but before long she was pregnant again, and

Henry's confidence was rewarded. On New Year's Day 1511, she gave birth to a boy, Prince Henry.

The king was overjoyed. Lavish celebrations began. The huge guns at the Tower of London boomed out deafening salutes. In the streets of the city, fountains were made to run with wine, so that ordinary people could drink the new prince's health. Processions and church services were held, and Henry went on a pilgrimage to a shrine at Walsingham to give thanks to God.

Now that Henry had an heir, he felt free at last to joust. The celebratory tournament held for the prince's birth was a glittering occasion. Henry took on the role of Queen Catherine's knight, Sir Loyal Heart. Riding a horse decked out in gold and blue velvet, he shattered lance after lance as he expertly struck his opponents. But his joy was cut short less than two months later. On February 22, the baby prince died.

It was another bitter February for Henry. In public, and with his wife, Henry maintained his dignity and assured everyone that more sons would follow. In private, he was wracked with grief.

One of the few who knew it was a butcher's son from Ipswich called Thomas Wolsey. Wolsey was a priest. By sheer brilliance of mind and hard work, he had risen to become the king's newest and most talented advisor. And when, one grey morning, the French ambassador tried to gain entry to the king's private room – his Privy Chamber – it was Thomas Wolsey who turned him away.

'When will His Grace come out and give audience?' asked the ambassador.

'My Lord,' said Wolsey, blocking the door with his portly frame and sweeping the Frenchman a dignified bow. 'I fear His Grace will not come out today at all.'

Like so many other noblemen at Court, the ambassador disliked having to deal on equal terms with such a low-born man. But he had no choice. Wolsey was gaining in power, Court rumour said, every day.

'But I have a letter from the king of France, expressing his sympathy,' the ambassador said stiffly.

Wolsey inclined his head. 'His Grace will receive it with great gratitude in good time. But I pray you, my lord, do not present it now. He is too deep in grief.'

The ambassador hesitated. Then he bowed reluctantly and retreated.

Wolsey strolled to the window. As he looked outside, a grim smile spread across his face. *And I dare not tell a Frenchman the only thing that will distract the king from his sorrow*, he thought. For that distraction would affect France deeply.

It was war.

8

'But, Your Grace, war can be avoided –'

'Think of the money saved, the men, the ships –'

The members of Henry's Council were trying to dissuade him. The king only glowered.

'Your father made peace with France,' another

councillor began. 'The French king is willing to renew the agreement –'

'Willing? The French king is *willing*?' thundered Henry, pacing the Council Chamber. 'Scared, more like! He dare not look me in the face, let alone make war on me!'

'Will anything change his mind?' said the councillors to one another when Henry, still fuming, had left the room.

Only Wolsey followed Henry out. 'War is the sport of kings, Your Grace,' he said, catching up with him. 'It is popular with the people – and with the nobles, too.'

Just like Henry, the noblemen at Court loved their tournaments, but what they longed for was the real thing. Henry kept walking, saying nothing.

Wolsey tried again. 'And taking France will bring you honour. You will be known throughout history as Henry the Great, ruler of an Empire.'

At last Henry stopped and turned to Wolsey. 'You alone understand me, Thomas,' he said. 'Let us win fame and glory. Let us conquer France!'

Thomas Wolsey bowed low before his sovereign. 'Whatever you wish, it shall be done.'

9

Wolsey set to work and preparations were made for an invasion of France. At last, on a fine June day in 1513, Henry and Queen Catherine said farewell to one another at Dover before Henry set sail with his troops.

Though anxious for his safety, Catherine supported Henry's ambitions wholeheartedly. And Henry had chosen her to be in charge while he was away. Catherine, he knew, had the talent and the character to be a strong, clever ruler.

She would need those qualities. Scotland – one of England's oldest enemies – took the chance while Henry was away to attack. Catherine assumed military command. Though she did not fight, she put on armour and led a large army northwards out of London.

Meanwhile, in France, Henry did not fight, either. He longed to lead the troops, and felt convinced that he would win glory if he did. But, still without an heir, the risk was too great. Instead, he got as close to the action as he could. When his troops surrounded a French city called Thérouanne and stopped food supplies coming in, trying to starve the city into surrender, Henry joined them.

While his soldiers camped without shelter, Henry had brought his life of luxury with him – he had huge pavilions made of cloth of gold and velvet, and a timber house to sleep in (made back home in kit-form, for easy assembly), complete with fireplace, windows and a magnificent canopied bed.

When, on August 16, the French cavalry were spotted approaching from the south, carrying great sides of bacon, which they hoped to deliver to the starving citizens, Henry mobilised his troops.

'Advance, in the name of England and St George!' he cried.

As his knights galloped forward to meet the French, and his gunners and archers let off bursts of fire, Henry stayed at the rear of his army, a safe distance from the action.

But still, when the French cavalry fled, dropping

their weapons in their haste and spurring their horses to gallop away, Henry claimed it as a personal victory.

'See how God favours my claim to France!' he exclaimed. 'The valiant French spurred their horses to run away, did they? Ha, ha! We shall call it "The Battle of the Spurs"!'

Back home in England, Catherine had a victory of her own. English troops met the Scots in battle at Flodden, and the Scots were heavily defeated. Their king, James IV, was killed, along with many Scottish nobles, bishops and more than ten thousand ordinary troops. Ecstatic, Catherine sent James's bloodstained coat to Henry in France as a trophy. The king was thrilled – it did not matter to him that James was his brother-in-law, the husband of his elder sister, Margaret.

Henry's return to England was triumphant. Though he hadn't conquered France, his troops had captured one city, destroyed another and beaten the Scots. However, the war had emptied the royal coffers. Henry needed money. As so often now, he found it was Wolsey who had the answer.

Out walking together in the orchard at Greenwich that September, Henry's trusted minister explained his plan.

'There is a solution Your Grace might consider,' said Wolsey, careful, as always, not to seem to instruct the king. 'We could make peace with the French.'

'Make peace?' Henry looked at Wolsey in astonishment. 'But we beat them in battle!'

'Exactly, sire,' said Wolsey. 'We have caused them such trouble, they will pay anything now for our friendship.'

Slowly, the king's astonishment melted into a smile. 'Thomas, you are as wily as a fox!'

And so Wolsey arranged a peace treaty between England and France. As part of it, Princess Mary, Henry's younger sister, was sent to marry the king of France, Louis XII – even though Louis was an old man in poor health. And in return for peace, France promised to pay Henry large sums of money.

'France bows to you – you are the finest king in Europe,' Henry's courtiers told him. 'There is no one to touch you!'

It was not long the case. Soon the elderly king

of France died. The crown passed to a young man called François, as athletic and ambitious as Henry himself, and – after the humiliation of The Battle of the Spurs – determined to reclaim French honour.

The finest king in Europe had a rival.

10

'This François – has he gone to war already?' said Henry, taking a cup of wine from a nearby servant.

It was just a few months since the new French king's coronation, and Henry was keen to hear every detail about him.

'He has won a great –' began a councillor, then stopped himself. 'I mean, a battle, Your Grace. In Italy.'

'He didn't fight in person, though?' said Henry airily, turning to look out of the window.

His councillors eyed one another. 'Ah, well, yes,

sire, he did,' another one ventured. 'Very bravely, apparently,' he added.

With a wave of his hand, Henry dismissed them. A moment later, they heard a crash that sounded like Henry's cup being thrown across the room.

Only Wolsey dared go back in. He had had an idea. He knew that, for Henry, political rivalries were very personal. And King François of France was not the only new rival Henry had. There was another young king in Europe – Catherine's nephew, Charles. Already ruler of the Netherlands, Charles was heir to Spain and Austria, too – he was set to rule vast territories.

Wolsey found Henry standing at the large bay window, staring moodily out at the gardens below. 'Your Grace, England is God's jewel among nations,' began Wolsey. 'But compared to the size of François's kingdom, or of Charles's lands, England is a small fish in a big sea.'

'Well, what of it?' said Henry, irritably.

'The population of France is six times greater than England's,' said Wolsey, coming to stand beside the king.

Henry shrugged. 'One Englishman is worth

six Frenchmen – more!'

'A thousand in your case, Your Grace,' said Wolsey, bowing. He went on, 'And then there is money. Charles, if he succeeds to his inheritance, will reign over such huge kingdoms, his income will be … oh, seven times greater than yours, sire, I should say. What power *that* will give him!'

'Thomas, do you seek to anger me?' Henry was scowling now.

'On the contrary, Your Grace,' said Wolsey. 'What would you say if I could show you a way to become just as powerful as either François or Charles?'

Henry looked sharply at his minister. 'How?' he snapped.

'You can turn *their* rivalry to *your* advantage,' said Wolsey smoothly. 'François and Charles will fight each other for dominance of Europe. But they will be evenly matched. Therefore, sire, *you* hold the balance of power – the one you choose to back will win!'

'Thomas!' exclaimed Henry. 'This delights me!'

'May I humbly suggest that I organise summit meetings with both men?' said Wolsey. 'Your Grace will astonish them with your personal magnificence, and they will see, too, how highly your friendship could benefit them.'

'Ha! They will be dazzled!'

Being so gifted at sports and horsemanship, Henry had always been lavished with admiration and praise. Neither François nor Charles could be so talented, he thought – could they?

11

Wolsey began to organise a meeting between Henry and François. It was a huge and complex task. At Hampton Court Palace – the most magnificent of Wolsey's private houses – he summoned his staff to the Council Chamber.

'The key,' Wolsey told them, 'is for England to prove itself France's equal – in wealth, in fashionable taste, in chivalry and accomplishments.'

Wolsey's staff were busy taking notes.

'I want this meeting to be an enormous, two-week party. Spare no expense!' said Wolsey. 'Let us have tournaments, jousts, ceremonies, feasts and dancing. Everything on display must be beautiful and expensive.'

Now he began walking up and down, seeming to pluck ideas out of the air. 'A temporary palace must be built for the king to lodge in. I will oversee the plans myself.'

'Yes, Your Grace,' said one of his men.

'Get the very best artists you can to design the heraldic displays. Get Holbein!'

'Yes, Your Grace,' said another.

'I want new delicacies served at the banquets. Get me turkey, asparagus, prunes…'

Wolsey's men could hardly write fast enough.

'I want fountains running with wine. Oh, and choose the ladies who will lead the dancing for their looks, rather than their rank. We won't let the French say our ladies are ugly!'

One of the most important decisions to make was where this great meeting should be held. Once, English kings had ruled large parts of France.

Now, besides the city captured in the recent war, England owned just one small area in the north, around the town of Calais. Wolsey arranged that the kings would meet on the border between this English territory and the French.

And so, in the summer of 1520, on a dusty plain near Calais, Henry's craftsmen created – out of nothing – a wonderland. On Wolsey's instructions, a huge temporary palace was built, outside which fountains flowed with wine. Around the palace, a town of beautiful pavilions grew up, to house the rest of Henry's Court.

Meanwhile, François's craftsmen had been equally busy constructing an equally extravagant display. So much expensive cloth of gold was used on both sides that the place became known as the Field of Cloth of Gold.

When Henry and François arrived, they were each accompanied by thousands of courtiers and servants, and their queens were accompanied by thousands more.

Meetings, banquets, dances and religious ceremonies were held. Gifts of eye-watering expense were exchanged. Everything was arranged to be equal, in order to maintain the pride of each nation. While Queen Catherine entertained François to a banquet at the English camp, Henry dined with the French queen at the French camp. While the two kings held a meeting, the two queens paid each other visits or attended a church service together.

Nevertheless, Henry, confident of his athletic prowess, could not resist challenging François to a personal competition. François was just as determined to beat Henry. Before long, in the name of sport, the two kings were preparing for armed combat in the specially built tiltyard.

'Give me my lance, man!' shouted Henry to one of his servants as he was helped onto his horse. 'It is ready to strike a royal target!'

Visors down, Henry and François charged at each other. Then again … and again. Each king scored points. Each king was an excellent jouster. But neither could beat the other.

Henry was not content. Later, when François visited his quarters, he said, 'Come, you shall wrestle with me!'

This had not been planned, but François replied,

'With pleasure.' He stripped down to his fine shirt.

Henry was strong. But he was used to wrestling with his courtiers, who let him win. Now François locked Henry in an unbreakable grip and threw him heavily to the floor.

The English courtiers held their breath.

'Ha! A fine move!' said Henry as he got to his feet. He was grinning. But he was angry.

Biting back his temper, he put a hand on François's shoulder and said, 'Let us take some wine! And then we shall have an archery contest!'

To the English courtiers' relief, Henry beat François at archery. But at the end of the summit – after two and a half weeks of ceremony, sporting contests and formal feasts – there had been no overall winner. Henry, François, their queens and courtiers were evenly matched – in money spent, food eaten, clothes worn and sport played.

In a final farewell ceremony, Henry and François made vows of eternal friendship. However, these vows were no more lasting than the magnificent palace Henry had stayed in. Before he had even crossed the Channel back to England, Henry held a meeting with François's great rival, Charles.

Henry VIII

Henry wanted to keep both François and Charles guessing – and he wanted to see which friendship would give England the biggest advantage.

That is how, less than two years later, Henry was at war with France again, in alliance with Charles.

By now Charles had become an Emperor, adding German territories to his huge kingdoms. Although this campaign in France fizzled out for lack of money and troops, Henry did not give up his hope of conquering the country one day. He believed he had proved himself the third great power in Europe, and equal to François and Charles.

There was one vitally important way, however, in which he was not their equal. Charles was not married yet, but François had an advantage Henry was acutely aware of – François had sons.

12

By the beginning of 1525, Queen Catherine was in her fortieth year. She had been Queen of England for almost sixteen years and was immensely popular with the people. Gracious and cheerful, dedicated to supporting her husband in all his endeavours and skilled at organising his life to run as smoothly as possible, she was seen as the perfect wife and queen. There was only one area in which she had not fulfilled her duties – she had not produced sons.

Catherine had been pregnant seven times, but only one child had survived – a girl, Princess Mary, who was now a bright, graceful eight year old.

As each year had passed, Henry had become more and more concerned. And, at last, it seemed certain that Catherine was beyond childbearing age. Yet Henry could not accept that Princess Mary was his only heir.

Now it was the day of a great tournament at Greenwich Palace, and Henry was preparing to take part. As his servants helped him into his armour, Queen Catherine carried on a conversation that was beginning – in its repeated revivals – to cause friction between them.

'My mother was Queen of Castile in her own right,' said Catherine. 'And she was a strong ruler, too. Why will you not accept that Mary can rule England as its queen?'

Henry slapped a groom on the side of the head as the man pulled a buckle too tight. 'Spain may be content to bow to a woman,' he said. 'But study your history books, madam. The last time a woman tried to rule England, there was civil war.'

Catherine knew all too well the story of Queen Matilda, who had ruled England for only a few months. 'Well then, my lord, we can arrange a glittering marriage for Mary, and she will rule alongside her husband,' she said mildly.

'Then England will become part of her husband's kingdom.' Henry planted his legs apart so that his leg armour could be strapped on. 'The English people will not stand for *that*!'

'So what is the answer? What else can be done, my lord?'

Henry did not reply, grumbling instead at his servants for their clumsiness. One of his legs had been sore ever since a heavy fall from his horse the year before.

'My lord?' Catherine tried again.

'Leave me, now!' Henry snapped. 'Can you not see that I am busy?'

It was new, this tone he used with her – the ease with which he dismissed her concerns. But Catherine had the self-control not to respond. With dignity, she curtsied and left.

When Henry was strapped into every piece of his heavy suit bar the helm, he clanked through the doorway of his chamber and beckoned to Wolsey, who was waiting outside.

Wolsey was now a very important priest – a cardinal. He wore a luxurious red robe and a short cape of velvet around his shoulders. His pudgy fingers glittered with expensive rings.

'Thomas, she will never give me sons,' said Henry as they walked together down the passageway. 'Why has God done this to me? He must be displeased with the marriage. Do you remember, some said that a man should not marry his brother's widow?'

'But the Pope gave you a dispensation, sire,' said Wolsey.

They came out into a courtyard where the king's horse was waiting. Henry greeted the animal and eyed with approval the gold-embroidered cloth that covered its haunches. Then he turned to Wolsey with a grim look. 'Perhaps, Thomas, the Pope was wrong.'

Out in the tiltyard, as the buzz of excited conversation sounded across the packed grandstand, Thomas Wolsey settled into his seat alongside one of his assistants. This man was clever and ambitious like his master and, also like his master, he was called Thomas – Thomas Cromwell.

Keeping his eyes on the colourful scene before them, Wolsey leaned towards Cromwell and said in a low voice, 'The king is having doubts about his marriage.'

Already an experienced courtier, Cromwell did not allow even the tiniest flicker of reaction to pass across his face. Instead, in equally low tones, he replied, 'He will put aside the queen and take a new wife, then, my lord? This is an opportunity to make a political alliance.'

'Indeed.'

'What would be the best choice? A French princess?'

'If we can find one to his liking, yes. It would be another way to press the king's claim to the French throne.'

Their conversation was interrupted by a fanfare of trumpets. Six fully armed knights entered the tiltyard on horseback, ready to defend the 'White Castle' – an elaborate mock-castle built in one corner of the yard. Standing on the castle's wooden battlements were four maidens – four of the prettiest ladies of the Court.

When the fanfare had finished, Cromwell said, 'But can we be certain the Pope will give the king an annulment?'

An annulment was a declaration that two people had never been properly married. If the Pope granted Henry and Catherine an annulment, Henry would be free to marry someone else.

'That,' replied Wolsey, smoothing his hands over his red cardinal's robes, 'is my task. I must make it happen. What the king wants, the king must have.'

'Sire ... here he comes –'

Two elderly knights entered the yard wearing silver beards and purple robes. Humbly, they asked Queen Catherine's permission to take part in the tournament, despite their age. The queen graciously granted it. Then the purple robes and false beards were thrown off. The elderly knights were in fact Henry and the Duke of Suffolk.

Henry enjoyed the gasps of recognition and delight from the crowd. He looked to see the reaction of the maidens of the White Castle. He looked for one of them in particular – a young woman with laughing brown eyes who had become the new star of his Court.

There she was, her dark colouring set off beautifully by her white gown, and the painted white-and-gold wood of the castle battlements. Those expressive brown eyes looked Henry's way for a moment, then lowered as she bowed her head in graceful acknowledgement of his gaze.

Henry was captivated by her. Her name was Anne Boleyn.

That day Henry fought as if he were twenty again, shattering lance after lance. The crowd clapped and cheered, astonished by his energy and skill. From their seats, Wolsey and Cromwell observed all this with sharp, knowing eyes.

'Well,' murmured Cromwell to his master, 'we may not yet know who His Grace's new wife will be, but I can take a guess at his new mistress.'

'Indeed,' replied Wolsey. 'No woman holds out long when the king begins to favour her.'

Cardinal Wolsey, however, had underestimated Anne Boleyn.

13

The king called Wolsey to see him in the bowling alley at Richmond Palace.

With a swing of his arm, Henry launched his wooden ball down the lane towards the jack. 'I hear that Mistress Boleyn has a sweetheart, Thomas,' he said, watching with satisfaction as his ball knocked two others out of the way. He dusted off his hands. 'Get rid of him.'

'Yes, Your Grace.' Wolsey bowed and hurried away.

At the palace's watergate, Wolsey stepped into his barge. He commanded the oarsmen to take him downriver to his house at Westminster. There, he immediately summoned the man in question, who was a member of his own household – the Duke of Northumberland's eldest son, Henry Percy.

Wolsey received Percy in the Long Gallery, an imposing room that looked out over the orchard.

The Gallery was thronged with servants. Wolsey knew that this lack of privacy would make the young nobleman uncomfortable.

Percy approached and bowed. 'You wanted to see me, my lord?'

Wolsey eyed him sourly. 'I am amazed at your foolishness,' he snapped, 'getting yourself involved with a silly young girl at Court – she is far from your equal in rank.'

Percy flushed. 'Anne Boleyn is from a highly respectable family, sir,' he replied.

'You are set to inherit one of the noblest earldoms in England,' said Wolsey. 'Your rank makes your marriage a question of State, on which it is your duty to consult the king.'

To his annoyance, Percy felt tears welling in his eyes. He could see what was to come. 'I am a grown man, my lord,' he said, swallowing hard, 'and perfectly capable of choosing a wife for myself. I have already promised to marry Mistress Boleyn. I cannot, and will not, go back on my word.'

'You are a wilful boy,' said Wolsey stonily. 'Well, I have summoned your father. He will make you break off your foolish match.'

Wolsey kept his word, and within two months Percy was forced to marry someone else.

Anne Boleyn was ordered to leave Court for a while. She was furious with Wolsey. She loved Percy and had wanted to marry him. As her servants packed her belongings, she stood at the window of her bedchamber. Below, in the formal garden, she could see Wolsey deep in discussions with his assistant, Cromwell.

'Thomas Wolsey, here is my promise,' whispered Anne. 'If it is ever in my power to do so, I shall take my revenge on you.'

Little did he know it, but Wolsey had made a deadly enemy.

14

With Percy safely married, Henry thought Anne Boleyn would soon become his mistress.

He began sending her admiring letters and expensive presents. But, to his utter astonishment, Anne remained unpersuaded. One moment she encouraged him to hope he might win her love – the next moment she brushed him off. Frustrated and tantalised, Henry felt himself falling deeper and deeper in love.

The months passed. When Anne was away from Court, Henry pined, longing to see her. His letters became more passionate. But when she returned, Anne still would not make a decision. She kept him in suspense for over a year.

Anne's older sister had briefly been one of the king's mistresses – Anne was not keen to add her own name to the list. But slowly an idea formed in her mind. She had heard rumours that Henry was thinking of putting Catherine aside and taking a new wife. Now she came up with an ambitious plan – to be that new wife herself.

At New Year 1527, Henry and Anne took a walk in the Great Garden at Greenwich, both wrapped in fur-lined robes to keep out the chill. Out here they had a little privacy. Anne seized her opportunity.

'I have made my decision,' she said, looking up towards the nearby tiltyard towers.

'At last!' Henry turned her to face him, his eyes bright and eager. 'Well?'

Anne smiled. 'I am yours, sire, heart and soul.'

'Heaven be praised! And body, sweetheart?' Henry slid a hand around her waist.

She stepped away. 'And body – *only* if I become your wife. I would rather lose my life than my honesty.'

For a moment, they faced one another in silence. Then they began to walk again.

'But how can it be?' said Henry. 'A king's marriage is a political alliance. A king does not marry for love – that is what a mistress is for!'

Anne stopped. 'In that case, I must ask you to forget me. Give me no more of your fine presents.

No suitors dare come near me while you are paying me such honours. No man can compete with the king!' She knelt before him on the cold stone path. 'Leave me to make a good marriage with some nobleman, as my father advises. Free me to do it, I beg you, while I am still young enough to bear my husband fine sons.'

Rising again, Anne began to walk briskly back in the direction of the palace, knowing full well the effect of her last words.

'Anne! Wait!' Henry hurried to catch up with her.

'My lord?'

'Anne, do not reject your king.' He swung round to block her path. 'I cannot lose you. I cannot be without you.' For a moment he hesitated – then he took both her hands in his. 'Anne, give *me* fine sons. We shall be married. I will make it happen, I promise.'

And, as the king bent to kiss her fingers, a glint of triumph showed in Anne Boleyn's eyes.

15

Together, Henry and Anne made a plan – to get Henry's marriage to Catherine annulled as swiftly as possible. Arrangements were made to hold a secret trial to decide the case. Catherine was not informed. Henry called a trusted lawyer to see him.

'Dr Wolman,' said Henry, as the lawyer knelt before him. 'I have summoned you on very grave business. My conscience is struck – God has shown me my error.' He reached for a jewelled copy of the Latin Bible, which lay on a small table beside him. 'Catherine and I are living in sin,' he said. 'Our marriage is against the law of God.'

Henry opened the Bible at a page marked by a fine ribbon. 'See here!' he said. 'It is written in the Book of Leviticus – *If a man shall take his brother's wife ... they shall be childless.*' He looked up again. 'This means without sons.'

'But, Your Grace,' began Dr Wolman, 'the Pope

gave you a dispensation –'

'The Pope was wrong,' Henry interrupted. 'I want you to argue the case for an annulment.'

'It would be an honour, Your Grace,' said Wolman quickly. 'I will set to work.'

In May 1527, the secret court opened in Wolsey's house at Westminster. With Wolsey sitting as judge, Henry and Anne were confident they would win the case.

The trial was due to last two weeks. In the final days, before giving judgement, Wolsey took some outside advice. He consulted John Fisher, the highly respected Bishop of Rochester.

'May I ask your opinion about a case of matrimony that has come before me?' said Wolsey, walking alone with Fisher.

Bishop Fisher nodded gravely. 'By all means, Cardinal.' He folded his hands inside his wide sleeves.

'The gentleman,' said Wolsey, '– I will not give you his name – has come to have doubts about his marriage…' Then Wolsey described Henry's situation, and his argument for annulment based on the Book of Leviticus.

'I know the Leviticus text, of course,' said Fisher, frowning thoughtfully. 'But there is another passage in the Bible which says that, if a man's brother dies before his wife has given him children, then the man *must* marry his brother's widow.'

'Yes, this is what has been troubling me,' said Wolsey. 'How can both texts be right?'

'Where no children were born in the first marriage, the rule of Leviticus does not apply,' replied Fisher.

Wolsey sighed deeply.

'Tell the gentleman, whoever he is...' Fisher stopped and put a hand on Wolsey's shoulder. 'If he wants an annulment, it can only be given by the Pope himself.'

'Thank you, Bishop,' said Wolsey, but his heart had sunk – he knew that Fisher was right. And that the king would not be pleased.

When Bishop Fisher had left and Wolsey was back in his Privy Chamber, a messenger arrived, carrying dispatches.

'I bring bad news from Italy, sire,' said the messenger, kneeling before Wolsey. 'The Emperor Charles's troops have run riot in Rome. They have burnt and ransacked the city. The Pope is the Emperor's prisoner.'

When he had dismissed the messenger, Wolsey held his head in his hands. This was the worst situation possible. Bishop Fisher had said that Henry's case had to be decided by the Pope. And now the Pope was a prisoner of the Emperor, Queen Catherine's nephew. All dreams of a swift and smooth judgement in Henry's favour had suddenly disappeared.

16

Wolsey's job was to get Henry what he wanted. So how, Wolsey wondered, could he persuade the Pope to grant Henry an annulment?

One thing was clear – with the Pope in the Emperor's power, the trial could not take place in Rome. So Wolsey wrote to the Pope, asking him

Henry VIII

to give permission for the case to be heard in England. He wanted the Pope to send a cardinal, armed with a document saying how the marriage could be proved invalid.

Though frustrated by the delay, Henry was still determined to marry Anne. The next step, he knew, must be to tell Catherine that their marriage was over. But he dreaded doing it. He respected her, and, after all, they had been married for almost twenty years.

At last, three weeks after the secret trial had collapsed, Henry went to the queen's chamber. There he found Catherine sitting with her ladies, sewing intricate black embroidery onto the collars and cuffs of his shirts.

Immediately, the ladies rose, and Henry commanded all except Catherine to withdraw to the next room.

'Dearest Catherine,' he said when they were alone. 'I must speak with you on a matter of great sadness.' He sighed deeply. 'Certain learned and pious men have come to me and broken the news that we are living in sin. I should not have married my brother's wife.'

Catherine's head lowered, and she began to cry quietly.

Henry took her hands. 'I know … you are as shocked as I was to learn this awful truth.'

'Truth?' Catherine looked up at him sharply. 'There is no truth in this, dear husband. I am weeping only because you are the victim of such evil counsellors.'

Dropping her hands instantly, Henry stepped back, his expression of sympathy gone. 'Perhaps it is best if you withdraw from Court,' he said stiffly.

Catherine shook her head. 'You may send me away, but I will never go of my own free will.' She curtsied. 'I will take advice on this matter, my lord, and we will speak of it again.' Then she swept from the room.

17

Thousands of miles away, in Italy, Pope Clement VII had received Wolsey's letter, asking him to give permission for Henry's case to be heard in England. Clement was living in a castle in Rome, but he was still Emperor Charles's prisoner. Now he was sitting in his private apartments, surrounded by a group of cardinals – his advisors.

'If you allow the case to be heard in England, Your Holiness,' one of the cardinals was saying, 'King Henry and Cardinal Wolsey will do everything they can to force a result in Henry's favour.'

'Would that really be so terrible?' another cardinal put in. 'Annulments have been granted to many other kings in the past, Your Holiness. If Queen Catherine would agree to retire to a nunnery, there would be no problem.'

'If you will excuse me, Your Holiness,' said a third cardinal, bowing, 'I must beg to say that this is not like annulments granted to other kings. The Pope before you gave special permission for this marriage to take place. King Henry is asking you to say that your predecessor was wrong. That is ridiculous. A Pope can *never* be wrong!'

The Pope raised one heavily ringed hand. 'Enough. A way around it *could* be found. If it were not for the Emperor, that is…' Wearily, he pressed his fingers to his eyes. 'The Emperor's troops have ransacked Rome. Now they are threatening my other lands.'

The truth was that Wolsey's request had put Clement in an impossible position. As the Emperor's prisoner, he needed the help of other rulers, and he wanted to please King Henry. But he also dared not anger the Emperor, who was Queen Catherine's nephew.

He looked round at his cardinals. 'I must delay my decision,' he said. 'Perhaps the Emperor's troops will be beaten back by the French. Perhaps King Henry will tire of this Lady Anne. Or perhaps Queen Catherine will die… If I wait long enough, something is sure to happen.'

The Pope's secretary, who was holding Wolsey's

letter, studied it again. 'He asks you to send a cardinal to England, sire.'

There was a long silence. The Pope turned the rings on his fingers. At last he nodded and said, 'Very well. I will send Cardinal Campeggio.'

The cardinal advisors frowned. 'Campeggio?' said one. 'But he is old, Your Holiness, and sick. He will have to travel more slowly than a snail!'

The Pope smiled. 'Yes, I know. What's more, I will give him a secret mission – to hold up this annulment case for as long as he possibly can.'

18

Cardinal Campeggio fulfilled his mission well. The journey to England took him several months, and even after his arrival he managed to make more delays.

Seven months later, in June 1529, the trial finally opened at Blackfriars in London. Henry and Catherine were called to attend. The trial chamber was open to the public and hundreds of ordinary men and women eagerly squeezed in. It was a marvellous chance for them to see the king and queen at close quarters. Henry was still a magnificent figure, although he was putting on weight from lack of exercise. The jousting wound he had suffered on his leg four years before had turned into an ulcer that would not heal.

Catherine had changed, too. She had lost her youthful bloom and, after seven pregnancies, she had become stout. But she was as smiling and gracious as ever, and there could be no doubt whom the crowds supported. As the queen made her entrance, many cheers and shouts of encouragement were heard.

'Care for nothing, Your Grace! Heaven favours you!'

Catherine had been queen now for twenty years. The people felt she had done a good job. Moreover, they didn't believe Henry really had doubts about his marriage – they thought he just wanted to marry Anne Boleyn.

Listening to the cheers for Catherine, Henry's smile froze. Through gritted teeth he said to the nearest guards, 'These are nothing but ignorant ruffians. Never let the common people into my palace again! Never!'

But, for today, the trial had an audience. And when he explained his side of the argument, Henry was very aware that they were listening.

'My conscience is in agonies at the idea that God is displeased,' Henry told the court. 'But if this trial judges my marriage to be lawful and godly, I will be delighted.'

At this, the onlookers whispered amongst

themselves. They knew the king was lying. Catherine knew it, too. When it was her turn to speak, she rose from her chair and, threading her way between the many lawyers and officials, she made her way to Henry's throne and knelt before him.

Twice, Henry tried to raise her up, but the queen insisted on kneeling. Then she said, loudly and clearly, 'Sir – pity me. This is not my homeland – I am a foreigner, and at your mercy. In what way have I offended you? As heaven is my witness, I have always been a true and humble wife. Search your heart, my lord – you know that we have been properly married.'

Her Spanish accent was still thick – but the crowds viewed her, with fierce loyalty, as their English Queen.

'My lord, I beg you to consider my honour, our daughter's and your own,' Catherine went on. 'Consider the reputation of my nation and my family, who will be seriously offended. Before you all, I appeal to the Pope. This case must be heard in Rome. It cannot be a fair trial otherwise.' At last Catherine rose to her feet. Then she curtsied very deeply to Henry and walked away.

'She is not returning to her seat. She is leaving!' said an official in surprise.

Henry commanded the court crier to summon her back.

'Catherine, Queen of England, come into the court!' called the crier.

Catherine kept walking, accompanied by one of her servants.

'Catherine, Queen of England, come into the court!' called the crier again.

'Madam,' said the servant gently, 'you are called back.'

'It matters not,' Catherine replied. 'I have said all I wanted to say.'

19

Catherine had made the speech of her life. The ordinary citizens were on her side more than ever, and the trial ground to a halt. Campeggio said that there should now be a break for the summer, and that the trial would reopen in October.

Henry was furious at the delay. Encouraged by Anne, who had long wanted to take her revenge on Cardinal Wolsey, he was furious with the cardinal, too. For many years, Henry had relied on Wolsey to get him what he wanted. Wolsey had made war – and peace – at his master's command. But now it seemed he could not get Henry an annulment.

The king was also becoming suspicious. Mysteriously, Catherine seemed to know all his plans. Every legal argument he prepared, she had an answer for. Every tactic he thought of, she knew how to frustrate, as if she had been warned in advance. Not knowing whom to trust, Henry suspected everyone – even Wolsey.

The fact was, among Henry's courtiers, loyalties were split. After twenty years, many felt strong ties of gratitude to Catherine. Though few would risk defying Henry openly, many dared help their queen secretly by passing her information.

Worse news for Henry was to come. While the trial was suspended for its summer break, the Pope declared it should not reopen in October – it should be moved to Rome.

Henry was outraged. Now Wolsey's enemies at Court – including Anne Boleyn and many of the nobles, who had long resented his power – saw the opportunity they had been waiting for. They persuaded Henry to sack the cardinal from his government job. They wanted Wolsey sent to the Tower, too, but Henry still had enough affection for him to refuse. Instead, Wolsey's houses and possessions were confiscated, and he was banished from Court.

One of Wolsey's enemies was Anne Boleyn's uncle, the Duke of Norfolk. Waiting in the Presence Chamber one day for the king to emerge on his way to Mass, Norfolk approached Sir John Russell, a courtier who knew Wolsey well.

'Do you think the cardinal expects to return to the king's favour, even now?' Norfolk asked him.

Sir John raised his eyebrows. 'The cardinal is an ambitious man,' he said. 'Brave, too. If he sees an opportunity, you can be sure he will step forward.'

Norfolk grimaced. 'By God and all the saints, I will eat him alive if he comes within ten paces of the king!' he snarled.

Norfolk and his allies were afraid that if Wolsey met the king, he would talk his way back into favour. They wanted to put as much distance between him and Henry as possible. Since Wolsey was Archbishop of York, they managed to get him sent to York. Wolsey delayed setting off for as long as he could. By the time he reached York, it was the summer of 1530.

But even York was not far enough away to make Wolsey's enemies feel safe. So they accused him of asking Emperor Charles and King François of France to put pressure on the Pope – not to give Henry his annulment, but to tell him to abandon Anne. Wolsey's plan, they said, was to make Henry realise only *he* was clever enough to sort out the problem, and recall him to power.

Hearing these accusations, Henry's anger was murderous. At last, he ordered Wolsey to be sent to the Tower.

Wolsey was terrified, but he set off south, travelling slowly. As the strain took its toll, he became increasingly unwell. The Constable of the Tower, Sir William Kingston, went to meet him halfway. By the time they met, Wolsey was so ill that for several days he could not travel.

Finally, the party set off again. When they arrived at Leicester Abbey, where they were to stop for the night, Wolsey knew he could travel no further.

As he lay dying, he said, 'If I had served God as diligently as I have done the king, he would not have given me over in my grey hairs.'

When news of Wolsey's death reached Court, Anne Boleyn knew she had her revenge at last. She and his other enemies rejoiced. The 'butcher's dog', as they sneeringly called him, was gone for ever.

20

At Christmas 1530, less than a month after Wolsey's death, Anne commanded her servants' livery to be embroidered with a new motto in French – 'This is how it's going to be, like it or not.'

Despite her defiant confidence, Anne was no closer to becoming queen. Wolsey had failed to find a solution to Henry's Great Matter – his name for the annulment case. Anne had suspected Wolsey of causing delay. But now that Wolsey was gone, no one else knew how to make progress.

Then Wolsey's former assistant, Thomas Cromwell, stepped forward. Cromwell was extremely talented; like Wolsey, he was ruthless, charming and incredibly hard-working. With his old master gone, Cromwell was determined to become the king's new favourite minister. He and Anne saw that they could work together.

At this time, people all over Europe were arguing

about the right way to worship God. One group, Catholics, supported the Pope. Another group, radical reformers, were against the Pope.

Though England was officially a Catholic country, Cromwell and Anne were both radical reformers. They believed the Pope should not have power over the Church in England. They showed Henry a radical book, which argued that a king should have supreme power over everything in his realm, including religion.

'This is a book for all kings to read!' declared Henry. He was excited. If he became Head of the Church in England, the annulment would not be in the Pope's hands, but his own.

However, Henry was afraid that if he annulled his marriage without the Pope's permission, Catholic rulers – such as the Emperor Charles – would use this as an excuse to attack England. So he hesitated.

The international situation was not favourable. For once, Charles and François were at peace, which meant Charles might have the time, troops and money to threaten England.

At home, there were more and more signs of opposition to the king's marriage plans, too.

To Henry's fury, notices appeared pinned up around London, criticising Henry and Anne. The Court was split between those who supported Queen Catherine and the old religious ways, and those who supported Anne and reform.

Henry and his advisers were trying different tactics at the same time. On the one hand, they carried on negotiating with the Pope. On the other, Cromwell began to work out how Parliament might be persuaded to pass laws that would make Henry Head of the Church in England.

Meanwhile, in the public world of the Court, Henry and Catherine pretended they were still a happy couple. They lived under the same roof – although they had separate apartments – they took part in Court ceremonies, and on feast days, they dined together. However, their real feelings were beginning to show through. Angry and upset at the loss of Henry's love, Catherine abandoned her usual tact.

'Your neglect causes me great pain,' she said to Henry one day, as their food was served. 'You do not dine with me on ordinary days, and you never visit my apartments.'

Washing his fingers in a gold basin, Henry replied irritably, 'I do not have time, madam. Besides, I cannot visit you as a husband because I am *not* your husband. All learned scholars agree.' He took the fine linen towel held out for him. 'If the Pope will not declare our marriage null and void,' he added, 'then I shall declare the Pope a heretic and marry whom I please!'

'Then my nephew and the Pope will join forces to attack England!' retorted Catherine.

There was a thunderous silence. Someone coughed nervously.

Catherine called for a drink, and was handed wine in a finely engraved glass goblet. When she had drunk, she said sweetly, 'For every scholar who supports your case, my lord, I can find a thousand to declare that the marriage is good and lawful.'

Henry had had enough. Pushing back his chair, he stormed from the room and went to find Anne. She was sitting with her ladies in her own grand chamber, playing cards.

'I cannot stand spending time with Catherine!' he exclaimed. 'She has an answer for everything I say!'

He bent to kiss Anne, expecting sympathy, but she turned her head away.

'Anne – no one else treats the king like this!'

She looked at him defiantly. 'Perhaps no one else is as wronged by the king as I am!' She slapped her cards down on the playing table. 'Did I not tell you that when you argue with Catherine, she is sure to have the upper hand? Some fine day you will give in to her arguments. Then what will happen to me? I'll be a cast-off.' Anne burst into tears. 'I have been waiting so long,' she sobbed. 'It is four years since you promised to marry me! I could have married someone else by now – I could have had children!'

Growling like a bear in a swarm of stinging bees, Henry left, crashing the chamber door shut behind him.

21

Despite Henry's anger, Anne knew that when she mentioned children, she was playing her trump card. Such talk made the king more determined than ever to marry her.

Though Anne was not yet queen, she decided it was time she took Catherine's place at Court. She persuaded Henry to send Catherine to live in the country. Catherine was also forbidden from seeing her daughter, Princess Mary. She was devastated. But for Anne, this was pleasing progress.

Soon came two more pieces of good news. François, King of France, agreed to sign a treaty of mutual aid with Henry. This meant that if Emperor Charles attacked either France or England, they would *both* fight back. And not even Charles was strong enough to fight both countries at once.

The other piece of good news was that Cromwell was making progress in finding a legal way to make Henry Head of the Church in England. With Henry's help, he made the Church give up its right to create church laws without the king's permission. Henry was now on the brink of being able to settle the divorce case himself. Cromwell had laws drawn up which – if Parliament passed them – would give the king that power.

But Henry hesitated again. So Parliament was postponed and negotiations at Rome continued.

Anne was frustrated. She knew that it would take something drastic to push Henry into giving up hope of an annulment from the Pope, declaring himself Head of the Church, and marrying her. So Anne took the most drastic action she could think of – she finally became Henry's lover. Soon she was pregnant with his child.

Henry was overjoyed. He felt certain that the baby would be a boy – his longed-for son – and that this showed God approved of his taking a new wife. But in order for the baby to be Henry's heir, Henry had to be married to Anne by the time it was born. Now, at last, he had to act – and fast.

22

In the chill mists of a late January evening in 1533, Henry was rowed in secret from Greenwich upriver to Wolsey's old house at Westminster – which had now become the king's palace of Whitehall.

The next morning, before most of the Court could even notice he'd been away, Henry arrived back at Greenwich. By then – unknown to almost everyone – something momentous had happened.

At Whitehall, Henry had met with Anne, two of his closest servants (who would act as witnesses) and a priest named Rowland Lee. A few days earlier, Henry had led Father Lee to believe that the Pope had granted a licence for his marriage. On this basis, Father Lee had agreed to perform the ceremony. But, much to Lee's concern, the marriage day had now dawned and he had still not set eyes on the document.

It was far from easy to challenge the king, but Father Lee said, 'Your Grace, I trust you have the Pope's licence?'

'What else?' said Henry, smiling.

'I would like the licence to be read, if you please,' said Father Lee.

Henry waved a hand. 'It is in another, more secure place to which only I have access. If I were seen to go and get it so early in the morning, people would be suspicious.'

Father Lee hesitated. He looked very uncomfortable.

Henry did not have much patience at the best of times. 'Get on with it, in God's name!' he snapped. 'Do your job!'

It was an instruction Father Lee dared not refuse. And so, in conditions of the utmost secrecy, he performed the marriage ceremony for King Henry VIII and Anne Boleyn.

For more than two months, no announcement was made. Rumours swirled round Court, however, and Anne delighted in dropping heavy hints that she was pregnant, and would soon be queen. At last, on Easter Saturday, Anne appeared for the first time in her new royal role. She accompanied Henry to hear Mass, dressed in cloth of gold and wearing the royal jewels. Even her supporters were dumbfounded, as Henry and Catherine's marriage had not been annulled. Still, nearly all the Court – terrified of angering Henry – took care to bow most humbly before their new queen.

By this time, the old Archbishop of Canterbury – the most important priest in the English Church – had died. The new man appointed to the job was a friend of Anne's called Thomas Cranmer. He was eager to help Henry and Anne.

Now Henry and Cromwell pressed Parliament into passing a law that made the king the highest legal authority in the country, even in religious matters. No case could be judged by the Pope. Indeed, to follow the Pope's rulings on any subject, religious or otherwise, was illegal.

At last, Anne had what she wanted. Henry had made himself 'the only Supreme Head on Earth of the Church of England'. Traditions of religious worship that had lasted hundreds of years were being swept away. This meant that Cranmer, the new Archbishop of Canterbury, could judge the case of the king's marriage – if he asked the king's permission first.

'I humbly beg permission to judge this case of your marriage,' wrote Cranmer in a letter to Henry.

'Permission granted,' came Henry's reply.

And so a completely new trial opened. It was feared that if it took place in London there would be riots, so it was held at Dunstable, deep in the countryside. Catherine refused to attend. With no one to put her side of the argument, Cranmer could do what he liked.

Not surprisingly, Cranmer declared that Henry had never properly been married to Catherine. The king's Great Matter was resolved – just in time for the coronation of Queen Anne.

23

On the afternoon of May 30 1533, a grand procession on the River Thames escorted Anne from Greenwich to the Tower of London.

The river was a blaze of colour. It was packed with boats and barges carrying nobles, bishops, the Lord Mayor of London and rich city merchants and tradesmen. One barge was decorated with a huge model of a dragon, which moved its head from side to side and spouted fireworks. Another was filled with musicians, whose playing could hardly be heard above gunfire salutes from ships lining the route, and above the boom of the great guns at the Tower.

The most magnificent figure of all was Anne herself, heavily weighed down with jewels, and smiling in triumph and delight. Arriving at the wharf, she disembarked and was greeted by a host of officials, led by the Constable of the Tower.

Finally, she was escorted to where the king was waiting for her. He kissed her, and led her inside.

Late the next day, Anne set off in procession again – but on land this time, carried on a litter through the streets of London. She was dressed in shining white, with her hair flowing loose over her shoulders, and a gold circlet on her head. Along the way, she paused to see short pageants performed. Their message was clear – she was a true blessed queen, and when she bore the king a son (as her large pregnant belly indicated she soon would) all England would enter a new golden age.

Anne thanked the performers graciously. This was a moment for her to savour – everything she had worked for over the past six years had been achieved. The woman Wolsey had called a 'silly young girl at Court' was about to be crowned Queen.

The procession took her to Westminster Hall. The following day, in the nearby Abbey, Anne – wearing royal purple velvet and ermine – was crowned. Afterwards, she sat in state at a banquet that lasted all day. Her dishes and drinks were served by noblemen; countesses stood nearby holding napkins for her to use. Many of them resented Anne's rise to power, but all paid homage to her, without a murmur.

No wonder. It was traditional for the king not to take part in such a banquet. But, set high in the wall of the banqueting chamber was a latticed window and, behind it, a familiar bulky figure stood watching.

24

Now that Henry had rejected the power of the Pope, he and his advisors watched the international situation with concern. Would any of Henry's 'brother rulers' use this as an excuse to attack?

Pope Clement had died by this time, and the new Pope – Paul III – wanted to give all Christians permission to seize Henry's throne from him. But Henry was lucky. Emperor Charles was busy fighting the Turks. And King François, who needed Henry's friendship – for the time being, at least – persuaded the Pope to delay his announcement. Still, Henry and his advisors could not relax. The threat of war would not go away.

Meanwhile, for a few strange weeks, England had two queens. It was only in the month *after* Anne's coronation that a proclamation was issued. Catherine was to be known now as the Princess Dowager of Wales – the title she had held as Arthur's widow.

Two days before this was made public, Catherine's household officers, headed by her chamberlain, Lord Mountjoy, informed her she must no longer use the title of Queen. Her daughter Mary was no longer a princess, either – she was now considered illegitimate, as if she had been born outside marriage.

Just as at the public trial of her marriage, Catherine knew the value of having an audience. She summoned all her servants to her Privy Chamber. There they found her lying on a daybed because she had hurt her foot with a pin. She also had a bad cough.

'Lord Mountjoy,' said Catherine weakly, 'please read the instructions you have received from my husband.'

Lord Mountjoy cleared his throat. 'Princess Dowager –'

'I reject such a title and always shall!' Catherine interrupted. 'I am the king's wife and the mother of his legitimate child and heir. I do not recognise the Archbishop of Canterbury's court or his verdict on my marriage.' She looked round the room at her assembled servants. 'If any one of you addresses me as Princess Dowager, I shall not answer you.'

Lord Mountjoy sighed. He had great sympathy for Catherine, but did not dare disobey the king. He had been told to send Henry a written report of this meeting. He hardly knew what to write.

When, with difficulty, he had drafted the report, Catherine insisted on seeing it. Looking at the document, she shook her head and snapped, 'Bring me pen and ink!' Then she crossed out the words 'Princess Dowager' each time they had been written, and inserted 'Queen' instead.

A group of Henry's councillors, headed by the

king's friend, the Duke of Suffolk, soon arrived to tell Catherine that the removal of her title was not all she was expected to endure.

'You are to move to Somersham,' Suffolk informed her.

This was a smaller, far less comfortable house, as Catherine and Suffolk both knew.

'What!' exclaimed Catherine, staring at the duke in disgust. 'That damp and pestilential place? I will not go. You'll have to bind me with ropes and take me by force!'

Suffolk bowed. 'That we will not do, my lady.'

Back at Court, Suffolk reported Catherine's reaction to Cromwell.

'She will not come out of her chamber, except to go to the chapel. She will not eat or drink anything unless it is prepared by her ladies in her own bedroom. For fear of poison.' Suffolk shook his head. 'She is reduced to a very low level.'

Cromwell merely shrugged. 'It is of her own choosing.'

25

The air in the king's bathroom was thick with steam and the scent of sweet herbs. When one of the royal councillors was admitted, at first the man could hardly breathe.

'Your Majesty,' he nevertheless managed to say as he knelt, 'news has arrived from Rome.'

Henry was reclining in a tub lined with fine cloths and soft sponges. His ulcerated leg was propped up on a cushion balanced on the rim of the tub, and another cushion supported his head. 'Oh?' he murmured.

The councillor cleared his throat. Giving the king this news was not a pleasant task. 'The Pope has declared your marriage to the Princess Dowager valid,' he said. 'He has declared your marriage to Queen Anne unlawful, and all children born from the union illegitimate.'

At this, Henry sat up with a splosh. 'A pox on

him!' he snapped. Then he sank back again into the warm water. 'But what do I care? The Pope has no power here.'

'No, indeed, Your Majesty.'

'However, some disloyal subjects may listen to him,' said a voice.

The councillor jumped. He had not realised that, concealed by the steam, Cromwell was sitting in one of the bathroom's window seats. 'They may plot against you, Your Majesty,' he added.

'How could any citizen of this realm *doubt* that my wisdom is greater than theirs?' This time the water slopped over the sides of the tub as Henry hauled himself onto his feet, wincing as he put weight on his bad leg. 'God has chosen me to rule over them!'

Servants ran forward with cloths to dry the king, and two of them helped him step out of the tub. 'Criticism of my marriage is a sign of one thing only,' said Henry. 'Wickedness. And the wicked must be destroyed.'

The councillor was dismissed. Swathed in towels, Henry moved to his dressing room with Cromwell in tow.

'Thomas,' began the king, approving with a terse nod the choice of a green velvet doublet, 'we must find the people who hold such evil in their hearts.' Henry disappeared for a moment as his shirt was pulled over his head. He was beginning to go bald. Emerging again, he said, 'Let us have each of our subjects swear a solemn oath. They must swear that they reject the Pope, and that they recognise my marriage and the legitimacy of my heirs by Queen Anne. Anyone who will not swear is a traitor.'

'An excellent plan, Your Majesty.' Cromwell bowed. 'I will have the oath drafted immediately.' And he left his sovereign to the nimble assistance of his dressers.

Radical reformers, like Anne and Cromwell, were delighted. But Catholics were appalled. Most of them were still loyal subjects of the king, who only wanted the old ways of worship restored. But Henry refused to accept this. He demanded total obedience, not just in people's actions, but also in what they believed.

'Each man must search his conscience,' said Henry's former Lord Chancellor, a lawyer named

Sir Thomas More. 'There is nothing more serious and binding than an oath!'

He was sharing a barge with Thomas Cromwell, travelling upriver to the palace of Whitehall. Cromwell looked out across the water to where the gardens of great houses lined the riverbank. 'I hope none will have a problem with it, sir,' Cromwell replied. 'Religious belief is not a private and personal matter – it is a matter of loyalty to the king.' He turned to look at More very directly. 'Anyone who does not swear the oath is the king's enemy.'

As Cromwell knew, More himself did not want to swear.

'But how can a person swear an oath when they believe it puts their soul in danger?' said More. 'When they believe it will make them go to hell?'

Cromwell did not answer. He knew what the king's remedy would be.

Henry's officials travelled round the country, commanding people to swear the oath. Most people, out of fear, obeyed. Those that refused were put in prison. Some were put to death.

Sir Thomas More refused to swear and was

beheaded. He had been a great friend of Henry's – but, just like Wolsey before him, More found that the king's love could quickly turn to hate if he didn't get what he wanted.

Amidst all this bloodshed, Henry was jubilant. He was certain that God's favour was shining upon him. And the birth of his son was about to prove this beyond all doubt – for the royal doctors and astrologers had assured Henry that Anne's baby would be a boy.

Henry had already started planning the celebratory jousts. And letters announcing the new prince's birth had been written, with a space left blank for the date.

At last, on September 7 1533, at Greenwich, Anne gave birth to her baby. It was a girl, and she was named Elizabeth after Henry's mother.

To both Henry and Anne, this was a heavy disappointment, though in public they pretended otherwise. 'Prince' was hastily changed to 'Princess' in the announcement letters, and celebrations were held. Henry's jousts, however, were cancelled.

26

James Needham, Surveyor of the King's Works, nodded and pointed to a spot on the large plan spread before him. It was the king's own design for new building work at Hampton Court Palace.

'Yes,' he said, 'Her Grace the Queen's jewel chamber and bedchamber are here – and here. And this door connects to Your Majesty's bedchamber –'

'And the new stair I wanted, leading to the garden?' demanded Henry.

Master Needham unrolled another large plan. 'Here, sire – Your Graces will be able to descend direct from your most private lodgings into the garden.'

'Very good.' Henry straightened up and nodded. 'The queen and I will come to see the work tomorrow. It had better be ready!'

Henry VIII

The lavish building project in progress at Hampton Court Palace was just one of many. Henry's expenditure was vast. Money drained away, spent not only on new buildings, but on furnishings, clothes, jewels, food and entertainment – and on fortifications and ships, to counter the new threat from abroad.

Henry needed more money – but he knew it would not be popular to demand fresh taxes. Besides, he had a new source of money available. For he was now Head of the Church in England – and the Church was rich.

A great part of the Church's wealth was owned by the monasteries. They were filled with treasures and valuable books. Above all, they owned vast amounts of land – three times as much land as the king himself. In 1535, Henry commanded Cromwell to report on the scale of the monasteries' riches.

Cromwell understood his master well. He told his inspectors to seize on any rumours they heard, however unreliable, about bad behaviour among the monks and nuns. Where there were no rumours, the inspectors made them up.

And so Cromwell's report, when it arrived, was

packed full of scandal. Henry persuaded himself that the report was entirely true – and was very shocked.

Most people agreed that a few monasteries needed to be reformed. Many kings before Henry had closed one or two, and used the money for charity or education. But Henry had much more drastic action in mind. He wasn't thinking of closing a handful of monasteries, he was thinking of closing hundreds – perhaps *all* of them. It would bring in a fortune.

Cromwell, loyal as ever, got to work on drafting the laws that would be needed.

27

One Sunday in early January 1536, Henry's usual procession from his apartments to the royal chapel to hear Mass was a peculiarly cheerful affair.

Today, Henry was dressed in yellow from head to foot, except for the white feather that decorated his expensive hat. Queen Anne, accompanying him, was dressed in yellow, too. And, behind them, the baby Princess Elizabeth was carried in state on a gold-fringed cushion.

The king was a picture of joy, smiling broadly at the courtiers who lined the chambers he passed through. 'Praise God!' he said to them. 'The Princess Dowager is dead! The Emperor has no reason to attack us now! At last we are free from the danger of war!'

The whole day was passed in celebration, with much laughter and dancing. Anne seemed supremely happy, but beneath her smiles lay a sense of unease. Some of her ladies-in-waiting understood why. As they sat sewing in the privacy of the queen's chamber, they talked of it.

'It is more than two years, now, since the birth of Princess Elizabeth,' said one of the ladies, named Margaret, 'and still the queen has not produced a son.'

'She has had a second pregnancy, though,' said another lady, Bridget.

'But it ended in miscarriage,' put in a third, whose name was Honor. 'To the king, that is as good as no pregnancy at all.'

Margaret nodded. 'The Princess Dowager's death must be a blow for her.'

'Oh – how so?' Bridget put down her embroidery hoop in surprise. 'She has often said what trouble Catherine caused, and how she looked forward to her death!'

'Ah, but…' Margaret sighed. 'While Catherine was alive, the king could never doubt his second marriage. For if he rejected Queen Anne, the people would demand his return to Catherine.' She reached for some thread. 'But now that Catherine is dead, if the king rejects Queen Anne, he will be free to marry again.'

On the other side of the room, Anne's sister-in-law, Lady Rochford, smiled confidently. 'Don't worry,' she said. 'The queen's place in His Majesty's favour is assured. She told me yesterday she believes she is pregnant.'

'Praise God!' said Bridget. 'Surely it will be a boy this time!'

28

Anne's baby *was* a boy. But he did not live. On January 29 1536 – the day of Catherine's funeral – Anne gave birth, far too early. The baby could not survive.

Not long after Anne's ordeal, Henry burst into her bedchamber. 'They have told me it was a boy!' he thundered. 'It was my *son*! Why could you not carry him safely?'

Weakly, Anne pushed herself to a sitting position. Her face was pale. 'My lord – your jousting accident,' she began hesitantly. 'It gave me such a fearful shock…'

Just a few days before, Henry had been knocked from his horse while jousting and had lain unconscious for two hours.

It was not an answer that pleased the king. 'You seek to blame *me*, madam?' he said.

'No, I –'

'Silence!' He looked at Anne coldly. 'When you have risen from your sickbed, I will come and speak with you.' Then he turned to go.

'You are unkind to me!' Anne blurted. 'I know about the presents you have given to other ladies –'

There was one in particular Henry had shown great favour to – a pale, mousy creature called Jane Seymour.

At the door, Henry turned to look at Anne once more. 'You must shut your eyes, madam, and endure as your betters have done. Remember – I have elevated you, and I can humble you again in an instant.'

As he stalked through the room beyond, Anne heard him add, 'I will have no more boys by *her*.'

Henry's cold fury terrified Anne. She hid her face in the pillows and wept.

'Your Grace, take heart,' said Lady Rochford, approaching the bedside. 'It is His Majesty's grief that makes him talk so.'

'No, no,' said Anne, lifting her head at last. 'Do you not see? He will do with me what he did with Catherine.'

Returning to his own apartments, Henry called Thomas Cromwell to see him.

Cromwell found the king brooding in his private library. A copy of the Bible lay open on the table before him.

'Thomas, I must speak with you in strict confidence,' said Henry, beckoning Cromwell to sit. 'God is displeased with my marriage, and does not permit me to have a son. I am beginning to realise that I was seduced into it by witchcraft.'

Candlelight threw Henry's bulky shadow, hugely magnified, onto the wall. 'Such a marriage cannot be valid, Thomas,' he went on. 'I believe that I might take another wife.'

Cromwell sat perfectly still, but in his head plots and strategies were already beginning to fizz. 'Indeed, sire, this situation must be a source of great pain to you,' he said. 'I will find a way to remedy it.'

Just like his old master Wolsey, Cromwell understood that his own power lay solely in giving Henry what he wanted.

Anne's fear that she would be put away like Catherine, however, was too optimistic. Catherine's refusal to co-operate had caused Henry lots of trouble. He did not want another ex-wife, causing trouble in the same way. Henry wanted to be *rid* of Anne.

Cromwell had his own reasons for wanting to destroy Anne. He and Anne had been allies, but they had fallen out over the plan to close the monasteries. Anne's anger, Cromwell knew, put him in grave danger. Anne had turned Henry against Wolsey – she could do the same with him.

There were many people at Court willing to help Cromwell, for Anne had plenty of enemies. They resented the land and titles that had been given to her family, and the way she had brought about Catherine's downfall and the reform of the Church. Anne had a quick temper, too, and had been rude to many courtiers she did not like. They had been waiting for a chance to turn Henry against her. Now it had come at last.

29

Jane Seymour – the mousy creature who had made Anne jealous – was the sister of one of Henry's favourite courtiers. Jane seemed to be the very opposite of Anne. Where Anne was fiery and argumentative, she was quiet and obedient. Henry was enchanted.

Eagerly, the Seymour family and Anne's enemies coached Jane on how to speak to the king, how to behave, how to make sure his interest grew.

While the glittering ceremony of Court life continued as usual, behind the scenes sinister events were taking place. On April 24 1536, Cromwell drew up a secret document. It appointed a team of nobles to investigate some unnamed matters – matters that might involve a charge of treason.

Then a handsome young Court musician named Mark Smeaton was arrested. On May 1, while the traditional May Day tournament was being held at Greenwich, Smeaton was tortured. The pain of the torture was so agonising that he confessed to having had an affair with Anne, even though it was untrue.

Cromwell was pleased. Smeaton's confession was a good start.

Henry and Anne were at Greenwich, watching the tournament together. All seemed to be well. Then, unexpectedly, Henry received a message from Cromwell about Smeaton's confession. The king said nothing to Anne, but rose from his seat and left. Though Anne did not realise it, Henry was leaving her side for ever.

Cromwell's activity quickened in pace. Several men, including Anne's own brother, were arrested. They were accused of having affairs with Anne, and of plotting with her to murder the king. The charges were ridiculous. But neither Henry nor Cromwell cared. They wanted to whip up public feeling against Anne, so that no one would complain when they got rid of her.

The next day, Anne herself was arrested. She was taken by river to the Tower. On another May morning, only three years earlier, she had come on this same river journey in preparation for her coronation.

Today, as then, the weather was fine, and great crowds had come out to line the river route. But they had not come to show Anne their support – they had come to witness her fall. The people of London had never forgiven Anne for taking Queen Catherine's place.

As at her coronation, Anne was greeted by the Tower's Constable, Sir William Kingston. This time, though, the king was not waiting behind him to embrace her. Instead, he was far away, enjoying the company of Jane Seymour.

'Mr Kingston,' said Anne, climbing gingerly up the damp and slimy steps, 'shall I go into a dungeon?'

The Constable held out his hand to steady her. 'No, madam, you will have the same lodgings as you did at your coronation.'

Suddenly overcome, Anne fell to her knees. 'Jesus, have mercy on me,' she said, and then burst into tears. A moment later, she began to laugh hysterically. It was a pattern that would continue throughout her imprisonment.

The trials of Queen Anne and the men accused with her were not designed to find out the truth, they were designed only to achieve a guilty verdict.

The accused were not allowed to have a lawyer to defend them. Anne herself answered the charges against her clearly and with dignity. None of them – except the broken Mark Smeaton – confessed to any wrongdoing.

It did not matter. The jury at each trial knew what the king wanted. And so, even though the charges against Anne and the men were entirely untrue, they were all found guilty and sentenced to death.

With great courage, Anne remained calm. 'I am resigned to die,' she said. 'But I regret that so many others – men who are innocent and loyal to the king – are to die with me.'

The usual sentence for a woman convicted of treason was to be burned alive. But Henry decided to give Anne a swifter and less painful death. She would have her head chopped off – and it was to be done not with the customary axe, but in the French manner with a sword. The executioner of

Calais – a man with a reputation as a very skilled headsman – was summoned specially.

The five men who had been accused with Anne died in front of great crowds on Tower Hill – a green space outside the Tower walls. The scaffold was built especially high, so that as many people as possible could see.

Anne was due to be beheaded two days later, on May 19. Her execution would take place more privately, within the Tower complex itself, on Tower Green. When the time for the execution arrived, Kingston escorted Anne to the scaffold.

Cromwell was there to watch, as well as Anne's uncle, the Duke of Norfolk.

Anne had been up most of the night, praying. She was exhausted, and almost relieved that the wait was over.

On the straw-covered scaffold, Anne's ladies stepped forward to help remove her headdress and her cloak. Underneath, she wore a grey gown, and her long black hair was held up by a white linen cap.

Anne knelt and tucked her dress in around her feet. Then one of the ladies blindfolded her.

She said, 'To Jesus Christ, I commend my soul.'

And, with one stroke of the executioner's great sword, her head was cut off.

30

'What a happy day, my beloved Jane!' said Henry, leading Jane Seymour out of the chapel room. They were at Thomas More's old house in Chelsea, and they had just been secretly betrothed. 'In little more than a week you shall be my wife!'

It was the morning after Anne's execution, but Henry did not feel a single twinge of guilt. He had eyes only for his new love – Jane. She was a slight, pale figure beside her king, and though his bald head was concealed under a jewel-encrusted bonnet, it was still clear that she was young enough to be his daughter.

But Jane had a determined set to her mouth,

and she wore the heavy royal jewels – so lately the property of Anne – with pride. This was a game with the highest possible stakes, and she had resolved to play it well.

One thing Jane had decided to do was to be a friend, as far as she could, to both Henry's daughters, Mary and Elizabeth. Elizabeth was still only a toddler, but Mary was now aged twenty – only a few years younger than Jane herself.

'I beg you to look kindly upon your eldest daughter, sire,' Jane said to Henry. She was well aware – though she did not dare say it – that Mary had long been unhappy.

But Henry was irritated. 'You are a fool,' he snapped. 'You ought to think of the future of our own children, instead of worrying about the welfare of others.'

'Oh, Your Majesty,' replied Jane sweetly, 'I am not asking for the good of others, but for your ease of mind. For the peace of the kingdom, too – and for the good of the children I will surely bear you.'

Henry smiled at this, and patted her stomach. 'I hope so, Jane. I hope so.'

Still, Jane could not save Mary from one of the most painful episodes of her life. Henry was determined that Mary should acknowledge in writing that she was illegitimate, that her mother had never been properly married to him, and that Henry was the rightful Head of the Church.

Mary was a devout Catholic. She believed the Pope should be Head of the Church. To declare her parents' marriage invalid was also a terrible betrayal of her dead mother.

On Henry's orders, Cromwell sent a group of councillors – led by the Duke of Norfolk – to the house in Hertfordshire where Mary was staying. They were armed with a list of demands, and they did not treat her gently.

'Will you accept the king as Supreme Head of the Church?' barked the duke. 'Will you admit that your mother's marriage was invalid?'

'Please,' Mary begged, 'for the love of God, do not make me sign any document. I am His Majesty's loyal subject and loving daughter – more I cannot say, or do.'

The Duke of Norfolk was unmoved. 'If you were *my* daughter,' he snapped, 'I would knock your head so violently against the wall that it would become as soft as baked apples!' He rolled up the list of demands and pointed it at her. 'You are a traitor, my lady, and you deserve to be punished as such.'

As Mary stared at him, aghast, the duke strode from the room. The rest of the delegation followed.

A few days later, Mary received a letter from Cromwell. She read it with horror. 'He says I must sign or suffer the consequences,' she told her chief lady-in-waiting. 'My supporters at Court are being questioned. Some are already in the Tower.'

'Your Highness,' the lady-in-waiting dared to say, though it was a title the king had forbidden, 'I urge you to sign.'

It was late at night before Mary could bring herself to do it. The candlelight flickered in the bedchamber as she sat at her desk – this young woman who had once been heir to the English throne – and signed a declaration that she had been born outside marriage, and that the Pope was not Head of the Church in England.

The news was brought to Cromwell. 'She is weeping constantly, my lord,' said the messenger, presenting the document. 'Her ladies had to stop her scratching her face and tearing her clothes.'

'Hmm.' Cromwell frowned. 'She has all the pride of her mother. But it was a sensible decision. She will learn to accept it soon enough.'

Now that Mary had done what Henry wanted, she was given fine new clothes, and Henry sent her a horse as a present. He also agreed to see her for the first time in five years. Obedience – total obedience in all matters – was what earned his favour.

Mary's surrender, though, had highlighted a matter of huge concern. Mary was not Henry's heir. Anne Boleyn's marriage to Henry had also been declared invalid, so Elizabeth was not his heir, either. Twenty-seven years after his first wedding day, Henry had declared all his children illegitimate. He still had no one to succeed him.

All eyes – and all the pressure – now turned to Jane Seymour. An Act of Succession, passed by Parliament that summer, said the throne would pass to Henry's children by Jane – *or by any wife that followed her*. How could she forget what had happened to Anne Boleyn?

At the end of September 1536, the date for Jane's coronation was fixed as October 29. But soon afterwards, the king had second thoughts. During supper in Jane's chamber, Henry asked whether she was pregnant yet – and when Jane said no, the coronation was postponed.

Later that autumn, anger over the closure of the monasteries in the north of England sparked a large popular uprising. First, the smaller monasteries had been closed. Now Cromwell was moving on to the large ones. The monks and nuns, condemned for their supposedly wicked lifestyles, were turned out. Their land, buildings and treasure were confiscated by the king. Thus Henry's wealth was vastly expanded.

The leaders of the uprising pleaded with Henry to restore the monasteries, to take back his daughter Mary as rightful heir, and to get rid of the advisors they blamed for all the religious upheaval – Cromwell and Archbishop Cranmer.

Henry was furious. 'How dare these traitors find fault with their king!' he stormed. 'They are no better than wild beasts and should be slaughtered accordingly!' And he meant it. Hideously cruel executions were carried out.

Queen Jane knelt before him. 'My lord, most humbly I ask – perhaps a *few* of the monasteries might be permitted to remain?'

'Get up!' barked the king. 'It is not for you to meddle with state affairs. Remember what happened to the last queen.'

31

In the summer of 1537, Henry turned forty-six. He had painful ulcers in both legs now. He continued to put on weight, too – which made his legs worse. Luckily, there was one piece of good news to improve his spirits – Queen Jane was pregnant.

On October 12, the longed-for event happened at last – Jane gave birth to a son, Prince Edward.

Wine flowed in the streets of London, two

thousand salutes were shot by the great guns at the Tower, bonfires were lit, and church bells all over the city rang out.

The baby was christened in great splendour, and honours and riches were heaped upon the Seymour family. But for Jane herself, triumph quickly became tragedy. Just like Henry's mother, she developed a fever for which the royal doctors had no adequate treatment. Twelve days after Prince Edward's birth, she died.

Henry had rejoiced in the deaths of his first two wives; this time he was plunged into grief. Now that Jane had given him a son, she seemed, in retrospect, the perfect wife.

Still, there were practical considerations. A single son – as Henry's father had known – was not enough. The search for Henry's fourth queen began within days.

32

Though Henry always noticed a pretty face, he was not (for once) showing serious interest in any of the young ladies at Court. So Cromwell was free to suggest European princesses and noblewomen who would bring with them useful political alliances.

England needed allies. The Pope had finally proclaimed that Henry was no longer the rightful king of England, and had sent messengers to Emperor Charles, King François of France and the King of Scotland, pressing for an invasion.

Moreover, François and Charles – after further fighting – had signed another peace treaty, which gave them an opportunity to act on the Pope's suggestion.

Henry considered a choice of at least nine different ladies. He sent his Court painter, Hans Holbein, to paint their portraits, so he could see if any of them pleased him.

Unsurprisingly, not everyone was keen to become Henry's fourth wife. One of the candidates, a beautiful sixteen-year-old widow, the Duchess of Milan, allowed Holbein to paint her, but made it clear she did not want to marry Henry.

'If only I had two heads,' she said, with mock regret, 'I would gladly put one of them at the King of England's disposal.'

And when Henry's envoy said his master was 'the most gentle gentleman living', it was all the Duchess could do to stifle her giggles.

Henry took a long time to decide which lady – and which political alliance – suited him best. At last, he chose a twenty-four-year-old German noblewoman called Anne, sister of the Duke of Cleves. Holbein's portrait so enchanted Henry that he could not wait to meet her.

But he *had* to wait. The overland journey from Cleves to Calais was slow. Then bad weather delayed Anne's crossing of the Channel. Waiting at Greenwich, Henry became more and more impatient – and his dreams of the bewitching charms of his new bride became more and more extravagant. He had never before agreed to marry a woman he had not met. It was tantalising, and exciting.

Finally, Anne's ship arrived at Deal in Kent. She began to travel, in stages, towards London. On New Year's Eve, she arrived at Rochester.

Henry could stand the suspense no longer. A romantic notion occurred to him – that he should set off on horseback to intercept her. What's more, like a knight in a story of chivalry, he decided to appear at his first meeting with Anne in disguise. So Henry and his companions put on matching multi-coloured hooded cloaks, and set off for Rochester.

It was the afternoon of New Year's Day by the time Henry arrived at the Bishop's Palace, where Anne was staying. Henry sent one of his gentlemen up to her chamber.

'My lady,' said the gentleman, 'His Majesty the King's New Year gift has arrived for you.'

Anne had been watching a bull baiting outside her chamber window. It was rather entertaining. Reluctantly, she turned to the messenger. 'I ... thank you,' she said. She looked curiously at his strange cloak – perhaps it was an English fashion.

Henry VIII

She was expecting a jewel or some fine cloth to be brought into the room. Instead, five more gentlemen burst in, all dressed in the same strange cloaks.

'Lady Anne, we wish you a blessed New Year!' they declared.

Anne was surprised, and a little alarmed. She looked round questioningly to the lady-in-waiting she had brought from Germany. The lady shook her head in puzzlement.

'I send you good wishes, too,' Anne said to the gentlemen. Surely it was not proper, she thought, for a group of men to burst into a lady's chamber? Anne turned back to the window, hoping they would go away.

Far from it. One of the men – hugely tall and hugely fat – stepped forward and, to Anne's disgust, tried to kiss her.

'Sir! This is most improper!' she blurted in German, but of course he did not understand. She stepped away and determinedly turned to the bull baiting.

The fat man grunted with displeasure. Anne was aware of him out of the corner of her eye, standing gazing rudely at her. Then he turned and strode out of the room. Stealing a glance at the other gentlemen as they followed him, Anne wondered why they looked so worried.

A minute later, the group returned. The cloaks had been discarded. The tall fat man was now dressed in royal purple. He was, quite obviously and devastatingly, the king. As she sank into a deep curtsey, Anne wished the floor could open up and swallow her.

Henry had played a game any lady brought up at the English Court would have understood. He believed that he was different from all other men – that his royal magnificence shone through any disguise. An English lady would have known her role in the game – to be astonished, and look prettily bashful, but then recognise that one of her surprise guests was the king.

Anne of Cleves came from a very different Court. There, games like this were never played. Ladies were expected to be simple and serious, and not even to sing or play music. Anne had no chance of understanding the game. Anne had little chance of charming King Henry at all.

Henry conducted the rest of the meeting politely, but his mind was already made up. He left Rochester as soon as possible.

33

'Get me out of this marriage, Thomas!' hissed Henry as he sat in his private prayer room. 'I will not go through with it.'

Cromwell, hovering uncomfortably just inside the door, said, 'I regret it more than I can say, sire … but the wedding must take place.'

There was an unpleasant silence. Cromwell hurried to explain. 'If we offend the Duke of Cleves, he may make an alliance with Emperor Charles. And the bride has completed the arduous and dangerous voyage to England –'

'I am not pleased, Thomas,' Henry interrupted. 'If I must marry this … this *woman*, you will arrange an annulment as quickly as possible, do you hear?'

Cromwell folded himself double in the lowest bow he could manage, and hurried from the room.

Henry and Anne of Cleves were married in January 1540, and for a few months only those closest to the king knew how unhappy he was. However, by May Day, rumours were circulating.

After the usual tournament, there was a banquet at a mansion called Durham Place. It was one of the king's houses, but today the jousters played the role of hosts, with the king, queen, and her ladies as their guests.

The banquet was followed by dancing, but Henry, in pain from his ulcerated legs, was unable to join in. Far enough from the king to be safely out of earshot, two of the dancing courtiers gossiped about him as they passed each other in the stately sequence.

'They say he's been seen crossing the Thames in a little boat, at all hours,' muttered the man to his partner, one of the queen's ladies-in-waiting. 'They say he is visiting a woman. Is he in love again?'

The lady nodded, with laughter in her eyes.

'And I know who she is, too...' She looked across to where another lady-in-waiting was sitting. Her partner followed her gaze.

The object of the king's affections was a brown-eyed girl who was plump with puppy fat, exquisitely pretty and, at nineteen, thirty years younger than her royal admirer. She was a cousin of Anne Boleyn, and her name was Katherine Howard.

'Every day she is laden with new jewels and fine clothes,' whispered the lady-in-waiting. 'The king can refuse her nothing. And she does not stop asking!'

Henry's new love affair was bad news for Cromwell. Katherine's family, the Howards, were his enemies. If Henry married Katherine, they would gain great power. So, instead of moving swiftly to get Henry the annulment he wanted, Cromwell tried to persuade Anne of Cleves to learn how to charm her husband.

It was a fatal mistake. Henry had shown time and time again that he would stop at nothing to get what he wanted. Now he wanted two things – to be rid of Anne of Cleves, and to make Katherine Howard his wife.

At last, after delicate negotiations with the Duke of Cleves, Archbishop Cranmer granted Henry an annulment of his fourth marriage. For Cromwell, though, it was too late.

Despite the years of devoted service, Henry allowed the Howards to persuade him that Cromwell was a traitor. He was beheaded on July 28 1540. Henry – his conscience untroubled by the murder – chose the very same day to get married. Katherine Howard was now his fifth queen.

34

The king's weight – already vast – had increased alarmingly during 1540. In December, inspired by his love for his pretty young wife, he started a new fitness regime. He got up between five and six o'clock every morning, heard Mass at seven, and then went out riding until ten, when he came back for his dinner.

At first, Henry felt much better. But the following spring, he was struck down by a fever.

'Will the king not come forth today?' asked a gentleman in the Presence Chamber one afternoon. He had been waiting several hours to petition Henry about the purchase of some monastery land.

The Privy Chamber servant, to whom he had spoken, shook his head.

'Not even in his wheeled chair?'

'His Majesty's legs are bad again,' said the

servant. 'The pain is terrible, and his fever is high.'

Several rooms away, in the inner sanctum to which only the most privileged had access, doctors were clustered around the royal bed. From behind the brocade hangings, a voice sounded irritably – 'No! Keep the queen away. I don't want her to see me like this.'

Whispered conversations followed. A groom was sent to the queen's apartments to answer her loving message of enquiry.

Meanwhile, Henry hauled himself with difficulty onto one elbow, trying to see past the doctors. 'Where is Cromwell?' He fell back onto the pillows, his face flushed with the effort. 'Send me Cromwell!'

'It is the fever,' one of the doctors murmured.

The Gentlemen of the Privy Chamber eyed one another uneasily, each hoping he would not have to tell the king the truth. Finally, one plucked up the courage to say, 'Cromwell is … dead, sire.'

'The most faithful servant I ever had! Why did you trick me, making false accusations against him?' He yelled, as pain shot through his leg once again. 'You are plotting against me, all of you!'

In her apartments, Katherine received news of the king's ill health with relief. After some time spent examining her new jewels, she was now busy reading a letter and giggling over it.

Katherine loved being queen, and she loved being adored by Henry. But he was not an attractive man. The Court, however, was filled with attractive men – young, handsome and ambitious. And Katherine had decided to play an astonishingly reckless game.

35

Despite Henry's ill health, in the summer of 1541, the royal couple set off on a 'progress' to the north of England. It was the first and only time in his life that Henry travelled so far north. He did so as a show of strength to his people, and took with him a thousand armed soldiers.

After twelve months of marriage, Henry was still besotted with Katherine. On his return to Hampton Court Palace that autumn, he ordered that there should be a day of thanksgiving for the great happiness she had brought him.

The thanksgiving – complete with solemn church services – was held on November 1. The very next day, as Henry went to Mass in the royal chapel, Archbishop Cranmer handed him a note.

'What's this, Thomas?' asked Henry gruffly.

Cranmer could not reply. It was a terrifying job to be the bearer of bad news to the king.

After his servants had lowered him into his chair, Henry opened and read Cranmer's letter. There was a long silence. Cranmer held his breath.

'No ... no,' the king muttered at last. He looked up at Cranmer, his beady eyes like currants in his vast flabby face. 'I will not believe it. This is an evil, false accusation.'

This was not the reaction Cranmer had expected. 'But ... we must investigate, surely, Your Majesty?'

There was a heavy pause. Then Henry said, 'Very well. I would be happy to have it proved untrue.' He put one hand on Cranmer's sleeve. 'But do it in secret – I do not want the queen to know.'

Cranmer bowed low and departed. The letter contained an accusation that Katherine had had several lovers before she had come to Court. This was a serious charge. Any young woman getting married for the first time was expected to have had no lovers at all.

Investigations began immediately. People who had known Katherine at the time were questioned – some were tortured. Soon it became clear that the stories were true.

When the news was brought to Henry, he wept

bitterly and for a long time. At last the tears were overtaken by a towering rage. 'Bring me a sword so that I can slay her myself!' he shouted.

Cranmer, meanwhile, was sent to Katherine, to get her to confess. He found her in a pitiful state; a frenzy of fear and weeping.

'My lady,' said Cranmer. 'Try to calm yourself.'

Katherine was pacing the room, her hands plucking at her sleeves. 'How can I?' she said. 'I will die!'

Cranmer had planned to speak harshly to her – now he feared that this might push her into madness. So, instead, he said levelly, 'It is true that your faults are very great, and you *should* suffer for them. Yet the king will be merciful to you.'

At this, Katherine rushed towards him. She sank to her knees, clutching Cranmer's robe. 'Is ... is it really so?' she stammered.

Gently, Cranmer uncurled her fingers and held them. 'Your actions before marriage bound you to another man as his wife,' he said. 'So you have never been properly married to the king. You are in disgrace, madam, but you will only be sent away – nothing worse.'

'How merciful is His Majesty!' cried Katherine, kissing Cranmer's hands and beginning to weep once more. 'This is far more than I could hope for!'

But what Katherine did not tell Cranmer was that she had another secret. And this secret was far, far more dangerous.

36

If Katherine had thought her secret would stay hidden, she was wrong. More people were questioned and tortured, and soon it was revealed.

The secret was this – before and during the northern progress, at places like Greenwich, Lincoln, Hatfield, Pontefract and York, the queen had arranged night-time rendezvous with a man named Thomas Culpeper.

Culpeper was a handsome, ruthless courtier. He thought Henry would soon die, and saw

Katherine as his route to power. Even under hideous torture, Culpeper denied having been the queen's lover. But a letter Katherine had written to him was found, which made the passion of their relationship clear – it was signed 'Yours as long as life endures, Katherine'.

Katherine had been encouraged and helped in her arrangements by one of her ladies – Lady Rochford, the widow of Anne Boleyn's brother. Lady Rochford, having lost her husband and sister-in-law to the executioner, knew better than anyone the risks she and Katherine were running.

There was certainly no hope for either of them now. On November 12, Katherine was arrested and taken to the palace of Syon. She was allowed several rooms to live in, and a small number of servants, but her jewels and finest clothes were removed. Henry kept well away. As he had shown with her cousin, Anne Boleyn, he liked to put the greatest distance possible between himself and the nasty business of killing a queen.

In early December, Culpeper was executed, along with the men who had been Katherine's lovers before she married.

Meanwhile, great numbers of Katherine's relatives were arrested for knowing about her past but not mentioning it to Henry. The Tower of London became so crowded with prisoners that the rooms of the royal apartments had to be used as prison cells.

Finally, on Friday February 10 1542, officials arrived to take Katherine herself to the Tower. Two days later, Katherine was told she would die the following morning. When the king's councillors arrived to take her to the place of execution, she was so weak she could hardly speak. Lady Rochford stood on the scaffold while her mistress's execution took place, and then followed her to the block.

Katherine was just twenty years old, and had been queen for a year and a half.

37

Wallowing in self-pity over Katherine Howard's betrayal, Henry was eager to cheer himself up. He held a banquet, and had twenty-six young ladies seated at his own table, and another thirty-five at a table nearby. But none of them took his fancy.

Henry's health was poor. He wasn't well enough to take exercise and so, as he carried on feasting, he became still fatter. This made him feel even worse. Soon, however, news arrived from abroad that cheered him up immensely. King François and Emperor Charles were at war again.

Henry's dream, as a young man, had been to have many sons and to conquer France. Refusing to accept that he was now ageing and ill, he tried to recapture his youth. He had hoped that marriage to Katherine Howard would give him youthful vigour and sons. That had been a humiliating failure.

Now he tried to recapture his youth in another way – by attacking France.

Emperor Charles, who was prepared to forget Henry's treatment of his aunt Catherine when it suited him, was delighted to find Henry willing to help. In February 1543, Henry and Charles made a secret agreement to invade France. This gave Henry a new burst of energy and optimism. And he decided to get married again.

The Council Chamber at Hampton Court was flooded with morning sunlight when Henry stomped in, leaning heavily on the arm of Anthony Denny, one of his favourite servants. Henry's face was puffy, with puce patches on a sickly, yellow-grey background. The smell from his leg ulcers seeped through his bandages, even though they had been changed just an hour before.

'Gentlemen,' the king began, when he was at last seated on his chair, 'I desire company, but I have had more than enough of taking young wives. I have now decided to marry a widow.'

And he had made his choice. This time, Henry had not fallen head over heels in love. Nor, for the first time, was there any talk of needing a new wife to bear him sons. Though no one admitted it, Henry's health was clearly too poor for that.

He turned to Denny. 'Send for the lady.'

A few moments later, a tall woman with a pleasant, friendly face entered the chamber. She was thirty-one years old, already twice widowed, and her name was Catherine Parr.

Now, before the Council, Henry made his formal proposal. 'Lady Catherine,' he said, 'I wish you to be my wife.'

Catherine knelt. 'Your Majesty is my master,' she replied. 'I have only to obey you.'

It never occurred to Henry how difficult this decision had been for Catherine. It was not simply that he was a terrifying, all-powerful king who had ordered the murder of two of his wives. Nor that he was now physically decrepit. Poor Catherine Parr was already in love with another man at Court – Thomas Seymour, one of Jane Seymour's brothers.

Catherine believed Henry's proposal showed God's will for her, and that it was her duty to accept. Nevertheless, it had been an immense struggle for her to give up hope of marrying the man she loved.

The king, blissfully unable to imagine that any woman could have such doubts, married Catherine on July 12 1543, in his private prayer room at Hampton Court.

Sensible and intelligent, Henry's sixth wife could not have been more different from his fifth. Catherine helped nurse her royal husband, ordering from her apothecary plasters and sponges, olive-oil ointments and pastilles made from liquorice and cinnamon.

And Henry chose his new Queen Catherine, like Catherine of Aragon long before her, to rule England as regent when he was away on his military campaign in France.

Henry was no longer a dashing young warrior leading his troops. He suffered a bout of illness just before his army set sail across the Channel, and his legs were troubling him badly. He had to be winched onto his horse, and a section was removed from his suit of armour where his leg was too swollen to be encased in metal.

Nevertheless, Catherine obediently supported Henry's dreams of military glory. She went to Dover to see him set sail. And when his troops succeeded in capturing the city of Boulogne, no one sent Henry more ecstatic congratulations than his queen.

38

Henry returned from Boulogne in triumph. But the mood did not last long. Within a year, the military tide had turned. Though English troops were still in control of the city, they were receiving no help from Emperor Charles, who was busy elsewhere in his vast territories. Meanwhile, the Scots had won a battle on England's northern border, and the French were threatening to take revenge for Boulogne by invading England's south coast.

Henry and Catherine travelled to Portsmouth so that the king could oversee work on the coastal defences. He was having dinner with the Admiral of the English Navy on board his flagship, the *Henry*

Grace à Dieu, when the French fleet appeared. Henry hurried ashore, to the newly built Southsea Castle. There, from a tower top, he could watch the battle.

The councillors accompanying him talked to one another in low tones, not wishing the king to overhear them. 'The French fleet is huge – look,' muttered one. 'They have two hundred ships. We have only eighty. And a message just reached His Majesty a moment ago – they have landed troops on the Isle of Wight.'

'The local militia will fight bravely there,' replied another. 'And here our sailors have the advantage of their position. They have the harbour at their backs.'

'But there is no wind,' said the first man. 'Our ships cannot move. The French have oar-powered galleys –'

Suddenly, Henry's favourite ship, the *Mary Rose*, began tipping over before their eyes.

'God's blood!' exclaimed the king. 'What is happening? Is she hit?'

The councillors hurried forward. 'She must be, sire,' said one.

'Or were the gun ports left open after firing?' suggested another.

'No, look – a hit! On the hull, down by the waterline!'

The desperate shouts of the ship's five hundred men carried clearly to Henry and his councillors. Rescue efforts saved only a few – hundreds drowned, and the king could do nothing but watch.

39

The Battle of the Solent, as it was called, was a victory for neither side. Both the English and the French lost ships, and the French fleet withdrew.

The fighting continued, but it soon became clear that the struggle to defend Boulogne was costing too much, in both lives and money. So Henry made a peace treaty with France. He agreed to return Boulogne to the French in eight years' time, in return for a huge cash payment.

Henry needed the money. The fortune gained from closing the monasteries had been squandered on military campaigns that had come to nothing. His dreams of military glory – cherished since boyhood – were in tatters. And, in almost constant pain from his legs now, he was a sick, irritable man.

This meant that for Catherine, intelligent though she was, the role of queen was highly dangerous. Two years after their marriage, Henry commanded a large portrait to be painted of himself and his family. He was shown seated on a throne, with his hand on Prince Edward's shoulder, and with his daughters Mary and Elizabeth flanking him. At his left hand, seated on a lower throne, was his queen. But it was not Catherine. Instead, the ghost-pale, richly dressed figure shown beside him was Jane Seymour, who had been in her grave for almost eight years.

The portrait was a stark reminder to Catherine that a dead queen was far safer than a living one. She might be his current wife, but she was not his favourite.

What's more, power struggles among the king's

advisors – the members of his Privy Council – were about to entangle her like a poisoned bramble.

40

It was clear to everyone that Henry did not have much longer to live. Months or perhaps years – but not many. His son Prince Edward was still a small child. This meant that when Edward became king, one or more of Henry's councillors would rule on Edward's behalf until he was old enough to take over.

One group of councillors, the conservatives, preferred the old religious ways. Another group were reformers. Both groups desperately wanted power once Henry was dead. Each hated the other, and they knew it would be a fight to the death.

Since becoming Head of the Church in England, Henry had imposed a very personal mixture of

Henry VIII

beliefs on his subjects. Henry's Church was neither a Catholic Church without the Pope, nor a Church that had totally embraced radical reform. Henry had come up with his own mix of old and new ideas, and he expected his subjects to believe what he told them to.

Many of Henry's changes pleased the reformers – relics and shrines were destroyed, pilgrimages were banned (even though Henry had gone on pilgrimages himself in his youth), and the Bible was printed in English instead of Latin.

But Henry also approved the Act of Six Articles, which enforced six conservative elements of religious belief and practice. Reformers hated it. The king also sometimes changed his mind. Six years after an English Bible had been approved for everyone to read, a law was passed saying that only upper-class men and women were allowed to read it – and the women only in private.

Henry's mix of old and new ideas meant that Catholics who supported the Pope weren't the only ones in danger of being executed for their beliefs – reformers Henry thought were too radical could be executed, too.

Queen Catherine was a very devout woman, and a keen supporter of religious reform. Henry liked to talk about religion, and Catherine loved discussing the topic with him. However, she was so enthusiastic that sometimes she got carried away, and forgot how dangerous it was to speak her mind to King Henry VIII.

It was the spring of 1546, and Henry was at the palace of Whitehall, recovering from a bad fever. Queen Catherine made daily visits to her husband, and today found him in his secret study, to which his servants had wheeled him in his specially built invalid's chair.

As so often, the king and queen's conversation turned to religion. When Catherine saw Henry's face darken, she assumed it was only the pain from his legs.

At last, Henry said, 'Leave us now. We need to speak with Dr Wendy.'

Catherine kissed his puffy hand, curtsied and withdrew.

'Farewell, sweetheart,' said Henry, but when the door closed behind her, his smile melted into an ugly scowl.

While one servant ran to fetch the doctor, another told the king that one of his councillors, a bishop named Stephen Gardiner, wished to see him.

'Let him approach,' said Henry and then, when the bishop entered the room, he let out a growl. 'Stephen! I have had enough of her instruction! What a comfort it is to me in old age,' he added sarcastically, 'to be *taught* by my wife!'

Bishop Gardiner was one of those councillors who hated religious reform. He had heard rumours that Catherine was starting to irritate Henry. Now this opportunity to attack the queen was too good to miss. 'It seems to me the queen tries to push Your Majesty towards radical religious reform,' he said. 'It amazes me that she would do such a thing to her sovereign lord –'

'Indeed, sir!'

'And she being only a woman, too – it is an insult! It is as if she seeks to direct your power herself. It is as if she seeks to act as king!' Gardiner went on.

'By the saints, sir, you are right!' exclaimed Henry. 'Women before her have learnt they dare not meddle with the power of a king, or it is the worse for them!'

'Do I have your authorisation, sire, to make some investigations?' said Gardiner, rubbing his hands in eagerness. 'Shall we ... start with her ladies-in-waiting?'

Henry nodded. He was gazing out of the window, lost in a self-righteous dream. 'Yes. Find out what books she has. Take her papers, too!'

'It will be done.' Gardiner bowed and left.

Henry gripped the chair wheels as an agonizing pain shot through him. 'Where is Dr Wendy?' he hissed at a servant. 'By God, man, get him here!'

At that very moment, to the servant's relief, the doctor was shown in.

Thomas Wendy was a small, slight man, dressed in a black robe. He set to work quickly, administering a tincture of opium to the king. Then, with the help of four strong servants, he moved Henry to a daybed, and began to replace the dressings on his ulcers.

Calmer now, Henry whispered, 'I have had enough of meddlesome women, Doctor.' His eyes narrowed with vindictive pleasure. 'The queen will be investigated.'

The doctor worked carefully, applying an ointment made of ground pearls to the king's legs. 'Indeed, Your Grace?' he said blandly, but he felt a shiver of dismay.

'Her ladies will be questioned. All her books and papers will be seized. Then the queen will travel by water to the Tower.' Henry's eyes clouded dreamily. 'As others have done before her.' His attention swimming back to the present, Henry added, 'You must tell no one, on pain of death.'

Dr Wendy nodded. 'Of course not, Your Majesty.' But as the king slipped into sleep, and the doctor at last got up, he looked pained.

Doctor Wendy was not the only person at Court to feel sorry for Queen Catherine. The next day, one of her ladies-in-waiting discovered a paper lying on the floor of the queen's outer chamber, as if it had been dropped there by mistake.

'Lord bless us, what's wrong, Madge?' said the queen, as the lady came back into the bedchamber, where the finishing touches were being put to Catherine's headdress. 'You look as if you've seen a ghost!'

The lady could not speak, but passed the document with a trembling hand to her mistress.

As Catherine read it, all colour drained from her face. The paper set out the case that was being made against her. 'Who left this?' she asked.

'I do not know, Your Grace.'

'A true friend, whoever it was,' said Catherine. 'But what am I to do?'

The queen paced back and forth before the great fireplace, the document crumpled in her fist. 'The charges are already drawn up,' she said. 'The king's mind must be set against me. I will die like the others!'

Catherine's distress became so acute that she collapsed. Later, as she lay fully clothed on her bed, the lady-in-waiting who had found the document came and knelt beside her.

'The king, hearing of your collapse, has sent Dr Wendy to tend you. To send his own doctor is a sign of favour, surely? Be of good cheer.'

The lady stepped back to make way for Dr Wendy. He looked down at Catherine with evident sympathy.

'If the king has spoken to you about me,'

whispered Catherine, 'tell me, I beg you! What is the cause of his anger?'

'The king has sworn me to secrecy.'

Catherine caught his hand and pressed it desperately. 'You have the power to save a life, Doctor! More certainly than ever before in your practice of the healing arts! Please, have mercy on me.'

After only a moment's further hesitation, Dr Wendy leant forward to whisper in Catherine's ear.

Catherine nodded and then looked brightly at the doctor, blinking away tears. 'Dr Wendy,' she said, 'if I live, I will reward you faithfully. I know that you have put your own life in danger to help me.'

41

Assisted by her ladies-in-waiting, Catherine put on a fresh gown. Then, trying not to appear nervous, she made her way to the king's private apartments.

She was afraid that Henry would refuse to see her. She knew how other queens had been destroyed by being kept away from his presence. But, to her immense relief, she was admitted. She found him in his bedchamber, propped up on a mountain of gold-fringed pillows.

'I have a mind to talk of religion, Kate,' said Henry, smiling sweetly as a serpent and patting the bed to indicate she should sit. 'Tell me your opinion of the common people being permitted to read the Bible for themselves.'

'My dearest lord,' said Catherine, sitting as he wanted, 'I am only a feeble-minded woman. God, in his mercy, has given me a husband to instruct and guide me.'

Henry frowned. 'Not so, by St Mary! You have become a teacher, Kate, to instruct *us*!'

Quickly Catherine slipped to her knees beside the bed. 'Your Majesty, I beg your forgiveness. That was not my intention.' She had rehearsed this speech in her mind – now her life depended on getting it right. 'I discussed religion with you for two reasons only. Firstly, to distract you from the pain in your leg. Secondly, I wanted to learn from you. It is such a temptation, being the wife of such a wise man. I cannot resist it.'

At this, Henry's sour expression vanished. 'Is it even so, sweetheart? Then we are perfect friends again!' He held out one great paw-like hand and she took it, and laid her cheek against it, swallowing back tears of relief.

A time had been fixed the next day for Catherine's arrest. When the hour came, she was helping the king to walk, with painful slowness, in his private garden. A heavy tramping of feet on the gravel path made them both look up. The Lord Chancellor had arrived with a detachment of forty guards.

'Your Majesty, we have come on sombre business,' the Chancellor began, 'to arrest –'

'To do nothing at all, sir!' bellowed Henry, in such tones that the Lord Chancellor immediately sank to his knees on the uncomfortable gravel.

'F-forgive me, but I thought –' he stammered.

'Knave! Beast! Fool!' the king roared, snatching the velvet bonnet from the Chancellor's head and beating him with it. 'Get out of my sight, you idiot!'

Scrambling, the Lord Chancellor obeyed. Catherine could breathe easily again. But it had been a very close call.

42

In September that year, Henry's dangerous fever returned, although his servants told the Court that it was only a cold. The pretence could not last long. By December, as the winter closed in, the king lay at his palace of Whitehall with the life slipping out of him at last.

Henry VIII

Still, the bloodshed did not stop. Despite six marriages, Henry was leaving behind him only one legitimate heir – a nine-year-old boy. And, just like his father before him, Henry was obsessed with the idea that some powerful noble would try to prevent his son succeeding to the throne. So, even in his last days, the heads of those who had angered Henry rolled in the straw of the scaffold.

Finally, however, as Henry's world narrowed to his bedchamber, and as the room began to reek with the smell of death, power seeped from the king into the hands of others.

Anthony Denny (who was now a knight, and Henry's most important servant) and a small group of councillors closed their grip tightly on access to the king. Queen Catherine was kept away. Out in the public rooms of the palace, Henry's meals were served to an empty throne.

For weeks, Henry had refused to accept that the end was drawing near. But, very early in the morning of January 28 1547, it was clear that the crisis had come. Sir Anthony said softly to his sovereign, 'Your Majesty, the doctors tell me you must prepare for your final agony.'

'Send for...' The crusted lips parted and shut again, as Henry struggled to speak. 'Cra-Cranmer...'

Cranmer hurried to the king's bedchamber, ready to hear him make a final confession of his sins. But Henry had called his archbishop too late. By the time Cranmer arrived, Henry was no longer able to speak.

'Your Majesty.' Cranmer bent low over the dying man and took his hand, unsure whether the king could hear him. 'Give me some sign, sire, either with your eyes or your hand, that you trust in the Lord.'

Weakly, Henry managed to press Cranmer's fingers. It was his last act.

Though Court and country did not yet know it, King Henry VIII was dead.

Index